A Listening Heart

David Steindl-Rast

A LISTENING HEART

THE ART OF CONTEMPLATIVE LIVING

CROSSROAD · NEW YORK

1992

The Crossroad Publishing Company
370 Lexington Avenue, New York, NY 10017

Printed in the United States of America

Library of Congress Cataloging in Publication Data

Steindl-Rast, David.
A listening heart.

1. Spiritual life—Catholic authors.   2. Monastic and religious life.   I. Title.
BX2350.2.S695 1983   248.4'82   82-23602
ISBN 0-8245-0576-X

ACKNOWLEDGMENTS

"The Environment as Guru" originally appeared in *Cross Currents*, vol. 24, no. 2–3 (1973). Used with permission.
"Contemplative Community" originally appeared in *Benedictines* XXVI, no. 2 (1971). Used with permission.
"The Contemplative and Monastic Vocation" originally appeared in *Careers in Christian Ministry*,© 1976, McGrath Publishing Company, Falls Church, Virginia. Used with permission.
"A Deep Bow" originally appeared in *Main Currents* XXIII, no. 5 (1967). Used with permission.
Excerpts from FOUR QUARTETS by T. S. Eliot reprinted by permission of Faber and Faber Ltd.
Excerpts from FOUR QUARTETS by T.S. Eliot are reprinted by permission of Harcourt Brace Jovanovich, Inc.; copyright 1943 by T.S. Eliot, renewed 1971 by Esme Valerie Eliot.
Haiku from AN INTRODUCTION TO HAIKU by Harold G. Henderson. Copyright© 1958 by Harold G. Henderson. Reprinted by permission of Doubleday & Company, Inc.

Contents

INTRODUCTION 7

A LISTENING HEART 9

THE ENVIRONMENT AS GURU 15

CONTEMPLATIVE COMMUNITY 24

THE CONTEMPLATIVE
AND MONASTIC VOCATION 31

MIRROR OF THE HEART 57

A DEEP BOW 83

Introduction

A Listening Heart is a small collection of essays harvested from the life of a man of paradox. Brother David Steindl-Rast is a professed monk of St. Benedict. He is dedicated to togetherness in the space/time community of Mount Saviour Monastery. Yet he is also a hermit of the Benedictine Grange. He is a perennial person who gives present witness to the ancient tradition of contemplative Christianity. But he lives in the depths of modernity. He is a man of silence. Yet he is a pioneer of East-West dialog. Most of all, he is joyful. For he recognizes that "It is not happiness that makes gratefulness, but gratefulness that makes happiness." These essays are not words about prayer but a graced act of prayer. This is a man whose wisdom comes from doing the truth of the heart rather than merely analyzing it.

The keynote essay gives the book its title. It illuminates the nature of a religious attitude rooted in the heart, that "center of our being where we are most fully one with all that we are and all that is." It is here that we give over our being to a unique call of the Word and find the obedience and detachment for living by the Word.

In "Environment as Guru" the controlled environment of the monastery, a setting for the pursuit of the contemplative attitude by professional contemplatives, becomes the paradigm for our discovery of sacred order. Silence and asceticism not only dispel confusion but allow us to surrender to that listening awareness that hears "the universal harmony to which we hope to dance."

The essay "Contemplative Community" points directly to an experience of meaning found poised between the two poles of solitude and togetherness. In the inner world of recollection and mindfulness, doings are transformed into play and thus activity becomes meaningful. It is here that we become what we already are.

"The Contemplative and Monastic Vocation" repeats and restates many of the earlier themes but emphasizes the call of the heart that we hear at the depths of ourselves. It is in mystical moments that we learn to savor the world rather than manipulate and use it. The paradox of every vocation and especially the monastic lifestyle is that we must face the reality that we are most truly ourselves when we lose ourselves.

Haiku, an Eastern form of poetry, is shown by Brother David in his essay "Mirror of the Heart" as a reality method, a way to discover the still point of the heavenly paradox seen reflected in the mirror of humanity.

"A Deep Bow" completes the collection by pointing to the universal Eucharistia as the root of a listening heart. In gratitude we experience gift as gift and enter the cosmic celebration—a thanksgiving sacrifice at the heart of the Christian life.

The natural repetition that occurs among the essays was allowed to remain for each essay and brings new and fresh highlights. The universal sphere represented in this collection is perhaps the most complete symbol for mapping our spiritual journey through the labyrinth of life. This collection is offered to the reader with the words of William Blake:

> I give you the end of the golden string,
> Only wind it into a ball,
> It will lead you in at Heaven's Gate
> Built into Jerusalem's wall.

RICHARD J. PAYNE

A Listening Heart

The key word of the spiritual discipline I follow is "listening." This means a special kind of listening, a listening with one's heart. To listen in that way is central to the monastic tradition in which I stand. The very first word of the Rule of St. Benedict is "listen!"—"*Ausculta*!"—and all the rest of Benedictine discipline grows out of this one initial gesture of wholehearted listening, as a sunflower grows from its seed.

Benedictine spirituality in turn is rooted in the broader and more ancient tradition of the Bible. But here, too, the concept of listening is central. In the biblical vision all things are brought into existence by God's creative Word; all of history is a dialogue with God, who speaks to the human heart. The Bible has been admired for proclaiming with great clarity that God is One and Transcendent. Yet, the still more admirable insight of the religious genius reflected in biblical literature is the insight that God speaks. The transcendent God communicates Self through nature and through history. The human heart is called to listen and to respond.

Responsive listening is the form the Bible gives to our basic religious quest as human beings. This is the quest for a full human life, for happiness. It is the quest for meaning, for our happiness hinges not on good luck; it hinges on peace of heart. Even in the midst of what we call bad luck, in the midst of pain and suffering, we can find peace of heart, if we find meaning in it all. Biblical tradition points the way by proclaiming that God speaks to us in and through even the most troublesome predicaments. By listening deeply to the message of any given moment I shall be able to tap the very Source of Meaning and to realize the unfolding meaning of my life.

To listen in this way means to listen with one's heart, with one's whole being. The heart stands for that center of our being at which we are truly "together." Together with ourselves, not split up into intellect, will, emotions, into mind and body. Together with all other creatures, for the heart is that realm where I am paradoxically not only most intimately myself, but most intimately united with all. Together with God, the source of life, the life of my life, welling up in the heart. In order to listen with my heart, I must return again and again to my heart through a process of centering, through taking things to heart. Listening with my heart I will find meaning. For just as the eye perceives light and the ear sound, the heart is the organ for meaning.

The daily discipline of listening and responding to meaning is called obedience. This concept of obedience is far more comprehensive than the narrow notion of obedience as doing-what-you-are-told-to-do. Obedience in the full sense is the process of attuning the heart to the simple call contained in the complexity of a given situation. The only alternative is absurdity. Ab-surdus literally means absolutely deaf. If I call a situation absurd I admit that I am deaf to its meaning. I admit implicitly that I must become ob-audiens—thoroughly listening, obedient. I must give my ear, give myself, so fully to the word that reaches me that it will send me. Being sent by the word, I will be obedient to my mission. Thus, by doing the truth lovingly, not by analyzing it, I will begin to understand.

The ethical implications of all this are obvious. Therefore it is all the more important to remember that we are not primarily concerned with an ethical but with a religious matter; not primarily with purpose, even the most exalted purpose of good works, but with that religious dimension from which every purpose must derive its meaning. The Bible calls the responsive listening of obedience "living by the Word of God," and that means far more than merely doing God's will. It means being nourished by God's word as food and drink, God's word in every person, every thing, every event.

This is a daily task, a moment by moment discipline. I eat a tangerine and the resistance of the rind, as I peal it, speaks to me, if I am alert enough. Its texture, its fragrance speak an intranslatable language, which I have to learn. Beyond the awareness that each little segment has its own degree of sweetness (the ones on the side that was exposed to the sun are the sweetest) lies the awareness that all this is pure gift. Or could one ever deserve such food?

I hold a friend's hand in mine, and this gesture becomes a word, the meaning of which goes far beyond words. It makes demands on me. It is an implicit pledge. It calls for faithfulness and for sacrifice. But it is above all a celebration of friendship, a meaningful gesture that need not be justified by any practical purpose. It is as superfluous as a sonnet or a string quartet, as superfluous as all the ultimately important things in life. It is a word of God by which I live.

But a calamity is also word of God when it hits me. While working for me, a young man, as dear to me as my own little brother, has an accident. Glass is shattered in his eyes, and I find him lying blindfolded in a hospital bed. What is God saying now? Together we grope, grapple, listen, strain to hear. Is this, too, a lifegiving word? When we can no longer make sense of a given situation, we have reached the crucial point. Now arises the challenge that calls for faith.

The clue lies in the fact that any given moment confronts us with a given reality. But if it is given, it is gift. If it is gift, the appropriate response is thanksgiving. Yet, thanksgiving, where it is genuine, does not primarily look at the gift and express appreciation; it looks at the giver and expresses trust. The courageous confidence that trusts in the Giver of all gifts is faith. To give thanks even when we cannot see the goodness of the Giver, to learn this is to find the path to peace of heart. For happiness is not what makes us grateful. It is gratefulness that makes us happy.

In a lifelong process the discipline of listening teaches us to live by *every* word that proceeds from the mouth of God without discrimination. We learn this by "giving thanks in *all* things." The monastery is an environment set up to facilitate just that. The method is detachment. When we fail to distinguish between wants and needs we lose sight of our goal. Our needs (many of them imaginary) keep increasing; our gratefulness (and so our happiness) dwindles. Monastic discipline reverses this course. The monk strives for needing less and less while becoming more and more grateful.

Detachment decreases our needs. The less we have, the easier it is gratefully to appreciate what we do have. Silence creates the atmosphere for detachment. Silence pervades monastic life in the same way in which noise pervades life elsewhere. Silence creates space around things, persons and events. Silence singles them out and allows us gratefully to consider them one by one in their uniqueness. Leisure is the discipline of finding time to do so. Leisure is the expression of detachment with regard to time. For the leisure of monks is not the privilege of those who can afford to take time; it is the virtue of those who give to everything they do the time it deserves to take.

Within the monastery the listening which is the essence of this spiritual discipline expresses itself in bringing life into harmony with the cosmic rhythm of seasons and hours, with "time, not our time" as T. S. Eliot calls it. But in my personal life, obedience often demands that I serve outside the monastery. What counts is the listening to the soundless bell of "time, not our time," wherever it be and the doing of whatever needs to be done when it is time—"now, and in the hour of our death." "And the time of death is every moment," says T. S. Eliot, because the moment in which we truly listen is "a moment in and out of time."

One method for entering moment by moment into that mystery is the discipline of the Jesus Prayer, the Prayer of the Heart, as it is also called. It consists basically in the mantric repetition of the name of Jesus, synchronized with one's breath and heartbeat. When I repeat the name of Jesus at a given moment in time, I make that moment transparent to the Now that does not pass away. The whole biblical notion of living by the Word is summed up in the name of Jesus in whom I as a Christian adore the Word incarnate. By giving that name to every thing and to every person I encounter, by invoking it in every situation in which I find myself, I remind myself that everything is just another way of spelling out the inexhaustible fullness of the one eternal word of God, the Logos; I remind my heart to listen! This image might seem to suggest a dualistic rift between God who speaks and the obedient heart. Yet, the dualistic tension is caught up and transcended in the mystery of the Trinity. In the light of that mystery I understand myself as a word spoken out of the Creator's heart and at the same time addressed by the Creator. But the communion goes deeper. In order to understand the word addressed to me, the word I am, I must speak the language of the One who calls. If I can understand God at all this can come about only by my sharing in God's own Spirit of Self-understanding. Thus the responsive listening in which my spiritual discipline consists is not dualistic communication. It is the celebration of triune communion: the Word, coming forth from Silence, leads by Understanding home into Silence. My heart, like a vessel thrown into the ocean, is filled with God's life and totally immersed in it. All this is pure gift. It remains for me to rise to the occasion by all-embracing thanksgiving.

The Environment as Guru

What I wish to share with you is aimed at making you feel at home in a monastery. We might begin with the question: "What should this environment do for us?" Maybe some of you have never been in a monastery; perhaps others have spent most of their lives in one. But it might be worthwhile for all of us to ask ourselves, "What is a monastery actually?"

The easiest answer, of course, and probably the best, is to say, "Come and see!" And if one came quietly enough, one might find out much without any talk. If, however, we have to speak about it, I would suggest that a monastery is, first of all, a controlled environment, with all the advantages and disadvantages included in this notion. It's inevitably a somewhat artificial environment, for a particular professional pursuit.

We know there are controlled environments for other professional pursuits. The monastery is a controlled environment for the professional pursuit of cultivating man's contemplative dimension. Those who live in a monastery have made this their profession. They have made public profession of dedicating themselves radically to the task of cultivating that contemplative dimension, which in fact belongs to every one of us. If we call monks the professionals of the contemplative life, this does not mean that they are better at it than amateurs may be. We all know that very often, when you need your sink fixed, an amateur plumber will do a much better job than a professional. That someone is a professional does not mean that he or she is better at the relevant professional skills; but it does mean that one ought to try harder. When we say that monks are professionals, therefore, we are saying that they have accepted the responsibility of cultivating professionally what many enjoy merely as amateurs, the contemplative dimension.

But what do we mean by "contemplative"? If we follow our own particular tradition as Benedictine monks and trace the very word to its Latin root, we may come to see an aspect of contemplation that might complement those that stand more in the foreground of other traditions. I stress this because Father Damasus, the founder of Mount Saviour monastery, used to consider it of great importance; in our tradition the notion of contemplation hinges on the Latin word *contemplari*. The image and, originally, the reality that stands behind this notion, is that of the Roman augurs, who marked off a particular area in the sky, the *templum*. Originally, *templum* was not a building on the ground, but an area in the skies on which the augurs, professional seers, fixed their eyes in order to find the immutable order according to which matters here below should be arranged. The sacred order of the temple is merely the reflection of the sacred order above. The Reverend Father Damasus kept stressing the fact that contemplation consists in the bringing together of the two temples, as the *con* in *contemplari* suggests.

Along with this Roman notion there is the biblical pattern: Moses built the sanctuary exactly according to the vision shown him by God on the mountain. Again and again the

Bible stresses the faithful correspondence between the temple on earth and its heavenly exemplar. In this sense, Moses truly fulfills the role of the contemplative. And not by chance; what he attempted and what the augurs attempted springs from the same root. The contemplative gesture is deeply rooted in man's heart, in his longing for universal harmony. Throughout the ages man has longingly looked up to the harmony and order of the starry universe and attuned his heartbeat to its measured movement. *Measure* seems to be the basic meaning of the linguistic root from which stem not only cognates like temperature, temperament, template and temporality, but, of course, temple and contemplation. To measure one's step by a universal rhythm and thus to bring one's life into harmony with a universal order—this is *contemplatio* in our tradition.

To move in step, one needs to listen; to sight one's course, one needs to look. The monastery is, therefore, conceived as a place where one learns to keep one's eyes and ears open. "Listen!" is the first word of St. Benedict's Rule for Monasteries, and another keyword is "consider!"—literally meaning to lay your course by the stars. St. Benedict, the patriarch of Western monks, wants them to live *apertis oculis* and *attonitis auribus*, with open eyes, and with ears so alert that the silence of God's presence sounds like thunder. This is why a Benedictine monastery is to be a *schola Dominici servitii*, a school in which one learns to attune oneself to ultimate order.

But such an order means nothing rigid. That would be the great danger, that would be the trap into which one could fall, to conceive of ultimate order as static. On the contrary, it is profoundly dynamic; the only image that we can ultimately find for this order is the dance of the spheres. What we are invited to do, what we are to learn in the monastery, professionally, is to listen to that tune, to attune ourselves to that harmony to which the whole universe dances. St. Augustine expresses the dynamism of order when he says, "*Ordo est amoris*," which means that order is simply the expression of the love that moves the universe, Dante's *l'amor che muove il sole è l'altre stelle*. But the fact is that while the rest of the universe moves freely and gracefully in cosmic harmony, we humans don't. It costs us an effort to attune ourselves to the dynamic order of love. At some point it even costs the supreme effort of, yes, making no effort. The obstacle which we must overcome is attachment, even the attachment to our own effort. Asceticism is the professional approach to overcoming attachment in all its forms. Our image of the dance should help us understand it. Detachment, which is merely its negative aspect, frees our movements, helps make us nimble. The positive aspect of asceticism is alertness, wakefulness, aliveness. As we become free to move, we begin to learn the steps; to listen to the music, listen and respond.

Asceticism may thus be understood as training in detachment (negative aspect) for the sake of being in tune with universal harmony (positive goal). But if this harmony is to be truly universal, it must encompass all of reality. If contemplation aims at "bringing the two temples together," all of reality must become transparent to its innermost luminous structure, ultimate order must find its expression in space and in time. Asceticism must, therefore, cultivate its own environment, as well as its awareness of space and time, as a form of obedience to the environment as guru.

If I understand it correctly, the word *guru* means dispeller of darkness. Not in the sense that there is something good or light, and something that is bad or dark: two parts of reality. I understand dispelling of darkness in the symbolic sense of dispelling confusion. If it is the guru's function to dispel confusion—beginning with the confusion that there are two parts to reality—the result will be order. Only let us keep in mind that it is the dynamic order of life and love, the mysterious order of the great dance. The various traditions have developed a great variety of forms for learning to put one's life in order—into this order. Prominent among these forms is what we might call an environmental asceticism of space and time.

Both in our tradition and in others, asceticism of space, the training in detachment as it relates to any given place, centers on learning to be present where we are. This is the first step: how often do we fail in it! We are ahead of ourselves or are hanging behind; we are neither stretching out to the future that has not yet come, nor hanging onto a past that is no longer here—and yet, we are not in the present, either. We are here and not here, because we are not awake. To be present where we are means to wake up to this place.

In the Jewish-Christian tradition a classical *locus* for insights regarding the asceticism of space is the spiritual exegesis of the scene in which Moses confronts the Burning Bush. The voice out of the Bush calls to him, "Take off your shoes! This is holy ground." To take off one's shoes—this is the asceticism of space. To take off one's shoes means being truly there, fully alive. The shoes or sandals we take off are made from the skin of dead animals. As long as we wear them, there is something dead between the live soles of our feet and the ground on which we are standing. To take off this deadness means taking off that familiarity which breeds contempt and boredom: it means coming alive in primordial freshness to the place where we are.

At first it is a specific place, the sacred precinct, which we enter barefoot. But then comes the next step, the decisive one: you come to realize that wherever you take off your shoes, you stand on holy ground. "All around in every direction: Holy of Holies" (Ez. 45:1), a passage Father Damasus never tired of quoting to his monks. All you have to do is to "take off your shoes" and you will realize this. In the Benedictine tradition this insight determines the attitude required toward every detail of the environment. The Rule of St. Benedict is concise to the point of being abrupt, yet it devotes an amazing number of passages to the various parts of the environment: the architectural layout, the use of tools, the food and clothing of the monks, the furnishings of the monastery. The final proof comes when St. Benedict says that every pot and pan in the monastery should be treated like the sacred vessels of the altar. This means: "Take off your shoes and recognize that you are standing on sacred ground; this whole place is a temple."

Any place is sacred ground, because it is, potentially, a place of confrontation—confrontation with the divine Presence. As soon as we take off the shoes of "being used to it," and come alive, we realize: "If not here, where? When, if not now?" Now, here, and/or nowhere, we are confronted with Ultimate Reality. "In the fields or on a journey, in whatever place the monks may find themselves when it is time to pray, let them reverently bend their knees then and there," enjoins the Holy Rule. And thus the asceticism of place opens up toward the asceticism of time. To the here, the holy ground, belongs the now, the Kairos, the holy moment, the acceptable time, the today of which we sing in the liturgy over and over again. "Today, when you hear his voice, harden not your hearts"—a decisive passage. And this today is always.

Time is something entirely different in the monastic context from that which a chronometer could measure. Time is not ours. When T. S. Eliot says, "Time, not our time," he points toward true detachment from time. We claim to have time, gain time, save time; in reality time does not belong to us. It is measured not by the clock, but by when it is time. That is why bells are so important in a monastery. Not only because most monks cannot wake up without a bell, though no one will deny the importance of that. But the really important thing is that in a monastery we do things not when we feel like it, but when it is time. When the bell rings, St. Benedict wants the monk to put down his pen without crossing his "t" or dotting his "i." Such is the asceticism of time.

There are occasions when it is time for something, whether you like it or not. And if you come only five minutes late, the sun is not going to re-rise for you; it is not going to re-set for you; and noon is not going to come a little later because you turned the clock back. Those are decisive moments, around which the whole monastic day revolves—moments that the bell indicates, not just arbitrary time of some timetable someone has made up. Let all these bells which you will hear ringing remind you that it is time, not our time.

The moment we let go of our time, all time is ours. We are beyond time, because we are in the present moment, in the now which transcends time. The now is not in time. If any of us know what now means, we know something that goes beyond time. For certainly the future is not, it has not yet come; and certainly the past is not, it is no more. So we say, "Well, but now is." But, when is the now? Is it in time? How long does this now last? Assign the shortest span of time to the now—you can still divide it in half: one half for the future, one half for the past. Is the dividing line then the now? As long as it remains a span of time, you can divide it again and again, *ad infinitum*. And so we find that in time there is only the seam between a past that is no more and a future that is not yet; and the now is not in time at all. Now is beyond time. And we humans are the only ones who know what now means, because we exist, we "stick out" of time. That's what it means to exist. And all those monastic bells are simply reminders for us: now!—and that's all.

To work through this asceticism of space and time from confusion toward order, from darkness toward light—that's what we try to do at the monastery. Of course, we cannot claim to have accomplished it. To quote Eliot again:

> For most of us, this is the aim
> Never here to be realized;
> Who are only undefeated
> Because we have gone on trying...
> (The Dry Salvages, V)
> For us, there is only the trying. The rest is
>   not our business.
> (East Coker, V)

We are trying to enter into that asceticism of space and time, to open ourselves to the environment as the dispeller of darkness and confusion, thereby finding peace.

Our Latin tradition defines peace as *tranquillitas ordinis*, the stillness of order. Order is inseparable from silence, but this is a dynamic silence. The tranquility of order is a dynamic tranquility, the stillness of a flame burning in perfect calm, of a wheel spinning so fast that it seems to stand still. Silence in this sense is not only a quality of the environment, but primarily an attitude, an attitude of listening. This is a gift that each of us is invited to give all others: the gift of silence. Let us, then, give one another silence. And let us begin right now. Let us give to one another that gift of silence, so that we can listen together and listen to one another. Only in this silence will we be able to hear that gentle breath of peace, that music to which the spheres dance, that universal harmony to which we hope to dance.

Contemplative Community

C ommunity is always poised between two poles: solitude and togetherness. Without togetherness community disperses; without solitude community collapses into a mass, a crowd. But solitude and togetherness are not mutually antagonistic; on the contrary, they make each other possible.

Solitude without togetherness deteriorates into loneliness. One needs strong roots in togetherness to be solitary rather than lonely when one is alone. Aloneness is neutral; loneliness is aloneness which is cut off from togetherness; solitude is aloneness supported by togetherness, "blessed solitude."

Togetherness without solitude is not truly togetherness, but rather side-by-sideness. To live merely side by side is alienation. We need time and space to be alone, to find ourselves in solitude, before we can give ourselves to one another in true togetherness.

A particular balance between solitude and togetherness will characterize a particular community. But by "balance" we mean more than the "ratio" between time spent alone and time spent with one another; we mean an inner relatedness of solitude and togetherness that makes each of them what it is in a given case.

On one end of the spectrum lies a type of community in which togetherness is the goal that is sought above all; a particularly close-knit family, for example. We may call this type togetherness-community. On the other end of the spectrum lies a community totally oriented towards solitude, for instance, a community of hermits. Let us call this type solitude-community. Since in either case both solitude and togetherness are essential for true community, the difference is one of emphasis.

The spectrum is continuous, but the distinction is clear; in togetherness-community, togetherness is the measure of solitude; the members have a right and a duty to get as much solitude as they need for deep and strong togetherness. In solitude-community, solitude is the measure of togetherness; here the members have a right and a duty to get as much togetherness as each one needs to support and enrich solitude.

A human being cannot survive without community. Nor can one be truly happy unless one finds the particular type of community that will fulfill one's needs for solitude and togetherness. The process of matching one's personal needs with a particular type of community within the wide spectrum of possibilities is an essential part of "finding one's vocation." (Note that we bracket here the question of "temporary vs. life-long vocations"; "vocation" in our context means merely what one feels called to choose at a given time.) What do we mean by "contemplative life?"

By "contemplative life" we do not mean life in a cloister. Contemplative life as a "vocation" means a particular form of life in which, ideally at least, every detail of daily living is oriented towards recollection. By recollection we mean mindfulness, ultimately unlimited mindfulness, the inner attitude by which we find meaning. Contemplative life in this sense is a form of life designed to provide an optimum environment for radical search for meaning.

Meaning and purpose are not identical; (it is possible, for instance, to accomplish a purpose that has no meaning). When we comprehend the purpose of a given thing or action, we "grasp" it, we are in control. When we want to understand the meaning of a given thing or situation, it must "touch" us ("How does this grab you?" young people say); we are responsive, but no longer in control.

By grasping purpose we gain knowledge; by allowing meaning to take hold of us we gain the wisdom that is the ultimate goal of contemplative life. The two are mutually complementary; we must distinguish without separating them. The openness for meaning is joined to the pursuit of purpose through leisure.

Leisure is not the opposite of work; (we should be able to work in leisure). The opposite of work is play. Work is something we do to accomplish a purpose that lies outside the activity itself; once the purpose is accomplished, the activity ceases. (We polish shoes in order to have them polished, not in order to polish them; once they are polished, we stop.) Play is something we do because we find meaning in it, an activity which has all its purpose within itself. (We sing in order to sing, for its own sake, not in order to have sung.)

Leisure introduces into every activity an element of play, an element of doing whatever it be also for its own sake, not only to get it done. Thus leisure provides the climate in which one can be open for meaning. Contemplative life as a form of life molded by a radical search for meaning will necessarily be a life of leisure, ascetical leisure.

It seems possible to gain some insights into the ascetic elements of contemplative life by an analysis of the so-called peak experience. This term denotes a deeply personal experience of meaningful insight, often in a flash, always in a moment of leisure. The experience itself is totally unreflexive, but later reflection finds in it a series of paradoxes.

What takes place in the peak experience is paradoxically that I both lose myself, and yet I am in this experience more truly myself than at any other time. Expressions one uses afterwards to describe what happened may include: "I was out of myself"; "I was simply carried away"; "I completely lost myself in..."; and yet "I was more fully alive, more truly myself than ever."

Another paradox of which one becomes aware in the peak experience is the fact that one is at the same time alone (not lonely) in a profound sense, and yet deeply one with all others present or even absent. Often a peak experience occurs during a moment of solitude, out in nature, for instance, or even in the midst of a large crowd. In a concert hall a passage of music which touches me deeply may seem to single me out, as if it had been written and performed especially for me. On the other hand, even on the mountain top or on a lonely shore, my heart expands in the peak experience to embrace earth and sky and all living creatures. The paradox is simply that I am most intimately one with all when I am most intimately alone.

There is a third paradox implicit in the peak experience: in a sudden flash of insight everything makes sense; everything, life and death and the whole universe; but not as if someone had given us the solution to a complicated problem: it is rather that we are reconciled with the problem. For one moment we stop questioning and a universal answer emerges; or rather, we glimpse the fact that the answer was always quietly there, only our questions drowned it out. When I stop asking, the answer is there.

The three paradoxes with which we are confronted in the peak experience provide a key for the understanding of contemplative life: they are like seeds out of which the most universal ascetical practices of contemplative tradition grow. Out of the paradoxical insight that I am most truly myself when I lose myself grows the ascetical practice of detachment. Poverty or detachment aims at more than giving away what I have; I must ultimately give away what I am, so as to truly be.

The experience of being alone when one is one with all provides a key for the understanding of celibacy. The sister sustains the paradox which others experience only in a brief moment. She is alone so as to be truly one with all; or one could also say that she is so deeply united with all that solitude is paradoxically the only adequate expression for this unity.

Ascetical obedience is also rooted in the peak experience, in the insight, namely, that everything makes sense the moment I stop questioning, the moment I listen. Learning to listen is the heart of obedience; following someone else's commands is merely a means to this end. In the last analysis, we have only the choice between absurdity and obedience. *Ab-surdus* means "absolutely deaf"; *ob-audiens* denotes the attitude of one who has learned to listen thoroughly, to listen with a heart attuned to the deepest meaning.

The peak experience is a moment in which meaning strikes us, takes hold of us. Contemplative asceticism serves to support the monk's wholehearted search for meaning. It makes sense, then, that the structural paradox of the peak experience should provide a clue for understanding the paradoxical structure of ascetical practice. Contemplative life is basically the attempt to expose oneself to the meaning of any given moment (through detachment, celibacy, obedience) in unlimited mindfulness.

Solitude in Community

Contemplative community in the strict sense will be a community of people who support one another in that radical search for meaning that finds expression in ascetical tradition. However, solitude is an integral part of this tradition in all its forms. An emphasis on solitude is implicit even in the disengagement characteristic of detachment and in the silence characteristic of obedience; in celibacy, solitude becomes explicitly a key element of contemplative life. Contemplative community is solitude-community.

This means that in contemplative community the members live in community so as to protect one another's solitude both from deteriorating into loneliness and from being infringed upon by misguided togetherness. If there is one lonely person in the community, the others must ask themselves: "Have we supported her aloneness by the togetherness she needed?" Yet, each one must also ask herself again and again: "Have I respected the solitude of my sister or brother? Have I protected it against my own whims of togetherness?" We are the guardians of one another's solitude, to the left as well as to the right.

Solitude, however, is not an end in itself. The end is a community supportive of the ascetical quest for meaning; and this is to say that the end is a community of leisure, for only through leisurely living can we find meaning. The very reason why people join to form community of this kind is the mutual help they can give to one another in creating an environment in which leisure is possible. The leisure of which we are speaking is not the privilege of those who have time, but the virtue of those who take time. Contemplative community is solitude-community for the sake of leisure. To live leisurely means to take things one by one, to single them out for grateful consideration. And this is the essence of celebration. All other aspects of celebration are optional, but when everything is stripped away that can be stripped away, these two elements remain. Wherever someone singles out something (or someone) for grateful consideration, we have a little celebration. Celebration cannot and need not be justified by any purpose; it is ultimately meaningful. To live leisurely means to celebrate every moment of life. Contemplative community is solitude-community, which provides leisure to celebrate life.

The Contemplative
and Monastic Vocation

You will remember seeing pictures of cave paintings made by shamans who celebrated sacred rituals tens of thousands of years ago. Yet, it has probably never occurred to you that these shamans, men and women set apart from their communities by a personal calling and dedicated to communication with a separate reality, are prehistoric links in a chain that leads directly to monastic life as we know it today. And when I say we know monastic life, I mean that all of us do know something of its inner secret, regardless of how little we may know about its external forms.

We all know from personal experience, as I will show, the inner secret that has given rise to all the many different forms of monastic life. But what is more, we all are somehow fascinated by that secret. Sometimes we feel that fascination as an attraction, sometimes it frightens us, sometimes our feelings hover right between fear and desire. We are dealing here with a realm of life for which this double pull of our emotions is characteristic. We are dealing with mystery.

Sometimes the inner attitude by which we expose ourselves to mystery is called contemplative. Everyone knows that contemplative and monastic are closely related terms. Yet, there is a good deal of confusion, and we better clarify our vocabulary before we go any further. What do you yourself mean when you say contemplative? No matter how vague your notion, you are referring to a dimension of life that gives depth to our otherwise flat world of daily living. In our contemplative moments we stop, for once, using and manipulating the world around us. We simply savor it. And right away things, persons, and situations begin to reveal a mysterious depth of meaning, unsuspected, a little bewildering, but fascinating. This area of experience is part of everyone's inner life. Not all of us are equally sensitive in this area, and different people have cultivated their contemplative life to different degrees. Still, to be human means to be contemplative at heart.

What we call monastic is far less universal. The term monastic refers primarily to a lifestyle, one among many valid lifestyles. It refers to an environment, to the monastery or cloister, one among many valid environments. The monastery is meant to be a controlled environment, designed to foster in every way the contemplative experience. It is a professional environment, as it were, for people whose whole lifestyle is geared to a systematic cultivation of the contemplative dimension of life. The monastic cloister is a kind of laboratory or workshop in which monks or nuns serve as professionals of the contemplative life. That's why they are sometimes simply called contemplatives.

Now we must hasten to say that being a professional does not necessarily make one better than an amateur in the same field. A professional has taken on a public obligation to strive for excellence in his particular field. An amateur is dedicated to that field out of a strong inclination of his heart. Too often we think of a dabbler when one is called amateur. Only in sports has the term retained its original flavor. Only amateurs are admitted to the Olympics, for their dedication is without any ulterior motives. Unless the professional adds the loving dedication of the amateur to his pursuit, he will fall short. Yet, the fact remains that monks and nuns are publicly dedicated to contemplative living by what is called the ceremony of their monastic profession.

To be the professionals of contemplative life distinguishes monks and nuns not only from lay people, but also from other professional religious whose lifestyle is not monastic. It distinguishes them, but it does not separate them. On the contrary. In fact, the very term contemplative gives us a clue to the intimate connection between the professionals and the amateurs in this field. Father Damasus Winzen, the founder of Mount Saviour Monastery, and my own spiritual father, used to explain the term contemplative in a way that brings out a deep truth, regardless how accurate it may be etymologically. In the Bible, Father Damasus used to say, the idea of contemplation is illustrated by the story of Moses, whom God calls into the cloud of his presence on the mountain top. There Moses contemplates the mystery of God's sacred plan. Later, when he builds the Tabernacle as the place of God's special presence in the midst of his people, it is emphasized again and again that Moses arranged everything exactly according to the pattern that had been shown him on the mountain. Contemplation is, then, the bringing together of the two temples: the temple of God's mysterious presence in the Cloud of Unknowing, and the temple of His manifest tent-dwelling in the midst of public affairs. What matters is that the two must be perfectly matched: "On earth as it is in heaven."

Contemplation is, thus, not only the visionary ascent into the cloud that covers the mountain, although we tend to restrict its meaning to that phase. The second, equally important phase of contemplation is the descent into the desert, there to realize the vision step by little step. The two phases must become an integral whole if contemplation is to be fully realized. We are limited in the roles we are able to play in this process. Our talents vary. In the monastic profession the emphasis falls on looking for the eternal pattern shown us on the mountain top. All other religious sisters, brothers, and priests are, by their profession, dedicated to construction work down in the valley. However, the two are inseparable. The vision without its realization remains barren. Service without a clear vision is mere meddling. There is even a constant overlapping of roles, so that everyone must to a certain extent play both parts. But more about this later.

Now that we have clarified our basic concepts, it will be easier to talk about the secret that lies at the source of every new attempt in history to realize the monastic ideal. That ideal is conceived as an environment and a lifestyle by which we will be freed and stimulated to expand in our contemplative dimension. We must, therefore, focus on the contemplative moments in our lives to find, if possible, in our experience what lies at the root of the monastic quest. This is easy and yet difficult. It is easy because you need not rely on complicated explanations. You simply need to reflect on your own experience. But this is where the difficulty comes in. What kind of experience is it we should try to remember and get into focus? Our contemplative moments seem so elusive.

The kind of experience of which we are talking has been called Peak Experience by Abraham Maslow. This is a helpful term. Experiences like that stand out like mountain peaks in the landscape of one's inner life. They are exalted moments, even though they may be moments of great pain and sorrow. They are moments of high intensity in which our awareness rises above its normal level. They are peaks also in the sense that they are like mere points separated by relatively long stretches of going down and of going up again, relatively short moments in time, though they might be quite frequent if we became alert to them. The term peak also applies in the sense that our contemplative moments are moments of clear vision, just as from a peak we can survey the countryside all around. Not that this vision or insight could easily be put into words. We encounter an inexpressible reality that gives us an insight that goes beyond words. We encounter mystery.

Peak Experiences are the mystical moments in everyone's life. Yes, in everyone's. Let no one say, "Me? I'm not a mystic!" A mystic is not a special kind of human being. Rather, every human being is a special kind of mystic. We better believe this and live up to our vocation. There is no point in comparing your own mystical experience with that of famous mystics in history. Your own is as unique and irreplaceable as theirs. And besides, whether you like it or not, it's all you've got. We can only start where we are, not where we'd like to be. That's rather basic in the spiritual life. If the mystical experience is, by definition, simply the experience of communion with Ultimate Reality, also called God, then, surely, all of us are familiar with it. But maybe you are looking for it in the wrong place, as you are searching your memory. God is not only in Church. Mystical moments are granted to us in places and under circumstances in which we would hardly expect them. Or maybe you are looking too high up. The most glorious things are often found close to the ground, for what is weighty sinks down. Nor should we search our memories for big events. Are not the smallest things often the most precious?

I remember an evening many years ago. My two brothers and I had just come to this country. We had been shown around all day by our hosts, who were eager to show us the best and the biggest and the newest of everything. By now I've long forgotten all the great sights and all the big events of that day. Only one experience stands out clearly in my memory. We were dead tired and just about ready to fall into bed, when one of my brothers called from the bathroom, "Look at that. Wow!" He had filled the bathtub with hot water and was now adding cold. As hot and cold water mingled, the different densities of the currents caused a strange dance of shadows on the bottom of the tub. (You can try this sometime and see for yourself, though I won't guarantee you a mystical experience.) But there we stood, the three of us, for a long time totally absorbed in silent contemplation. That's all I can say.

What had happened? Reality had caught us unaware and had touched our hearts. We have to resort to images if we want to convey more than appears on the surface. And, indeed, there is infinitely more to it. You could express it by saying that a spark of reality happened to penetrate the asbestos armor of fear by which we shield ourselves most of the time from getting burned. And at that moment we stood ablaze with the great fire. "But where does the supernatural enter in?" someone might ask. "Aren't you moving in the merely natural realm of experience?" While I, too, affirm the distinction between the natural and the supernatural, my question in reply is: "Where do you draw the line between the two?" You cannot separate them. Wherever, therefore, we truly open ourselves to the full impact of reality and faithfully respond to it, we are in touch with Ultimate Reality. Wherever we drink from the stream we drink from the Source.

It might be best, therefore, if you put out of your mind just now any consideration of what is contemplative, or monastic, or mystical. Simply try to remember a moment that felt super-real. Chances are that you'll hit on a Peak Experience. But remember: an anthill is also a peak. It need not be Mt. Everest. For people, for instance, who live on a high plateau of awareness most of the time, the relative elevation of the peaks might not be so great. All I ask of you is to remember one of these moments in which reality touched you. Try to pinpoint it clearly and specifically in your memory. And now pay close attention to check if my analysis applies in your case. If it does, we have found in your personal experience a basis for the understanding of monastic life. That would be quite an accomplishment. For the moment let us look without bias at the experience itself.

Well, the chances are that in an attempt to relate what happened to you in your peak experience you will find yourself saying something like, "I was simply carried away. I was swept off my feet. I lost myself in watching that child trying to catch a minnow in a tidepool." You lost yourself. You were carried away. Yes, these expressions quite accurately convey the experience. And yet in the same breath you'll find yourself admitting that you were more truly present at that moment than you usually are. You'll admit that you were more truly yourself at that moment than at most other times. Here lies a paradox! When I am carried away, I am truly present. When I lose myself, I am truly myself. And it applies to your own experience, doesn't it?

But there is another paradox that should also apply, as long as you are focusing on the kind of experience we are talking about. Let us suppose for a moment that the particular experience of which you are thinking was one in which you were physically alone. Maybe you were walking all by yourself at the seashore; maybe you were hiding out in your tree house (some of our most important Peak Experiences happen in childhood), or in some adult equivalent of a tree house; maybe you were really up on a mountain peak or on a hilltop beneath the stars; or simply alone in your car. If you try now to recapture how being alone felt at the time, you might find that you were more intensely alone than at other times, yet not at all lonely. Your heart expanded and embraced everything around you, the great things and the small, every pebble on the shore and every star in the sky. Things near and things far, past and future, all found their place in the great embrace of that moment in which you were one with all. Wasn't that it? But that's another paradox: When I'm truly alone, I'm one with all.

You can also turn this around. Maybe your Peak Experience wasn't one in which you were all by yourself. Maybe it occurred in the midst of a big crowd, say, at a prayer meeting; or at a concert. In those cases the feeling of being one with all others obviously played an important part in your experience. You felt as if this whole throng of people were one heart and one soul. But there, too, you were alone in a very special sense. You were singled out, as it were, by, say, that passage of the music you heard. It spoke to you. It called you by name. You were put on the spot. You alone. And you begin to realize that to be one with all means being alone, all-one. Indeed, all separations are transcended at that moment. Even the separation between you as the one who listens and the music you hear. It is rather "music heard so deeply/That it is not heard at all, but you are the music/ While the music lasts," as T. S. Eliot puts it (*Four Quartets* 3:V). It's the same paradox, only in reverse: When I'm truly one with all, I'm truly alone. Have you not experienced it yourself?

In a moment we shall see how basic these paradoxes are for our understanding of monastic life. But first we have to focus on a final paradox implicit in our encounter with mystery, and this is how we experience it: at the peak of our Peak Experience everything suddenly makes sense. Your heart is touched and there is peace. Not that suddenly you found answers to all your questions. Not that all contradictions are suddenly reconciled. Not even your problems are solved. But you have hit upon something deeper than questions; more comprehensive than all contradictions; something that can support all problems without need for solutions. How strange. We usually think that we must trace our questions to the ultimate question to arrive at the ultimate answer. We are convinced that we must work our way through contradiction after contradiction to arrive at an ultimate reconciliation; struggle with problem after problem to find the ultimate solution. Yet, what happened here is something entirely different. For one split second we were distracted from our preoccupations with problems, questions, and contradictions. That child catching minnow in a tidepool, that line of a melody, that flash in our lover's eyes, did it. For one split second we dropped the load of our preoccupations and the super-solution, the super-answer is suddenly ours, in one great super-reconciliation of everything.

What paradox! When I drop the question, there's the answer. In fact, we might begin to suspect that the answer is there all the time, trying to get through to us, while we are too preoccupied with our questions. But what disproportion between cause and effect. Why should one moment of true looking or listening yield what no amount of grappling with problems can wrestle from life? Our experience itself suggests an answer to this question. When we watch carefully, we notice that the child, the music, the loving glance, teased us for a moment into saying "Yes" to reality, a very special "Yes." We were caught off guard. Our heart went out to this tiny fragment of reality and burst into an unconditional "Yes." But having said this kind of "Yes" to the humblest fringe of reality, we have implicitly affirmed all there is. By drinking deeply from the stream we have said "Yes" to the Source. That is why our humble encounter is truly mystical, truly an experience of communion with Ultimate Reality. And since Ultimate Reality is the very "coincidence of opposites," we should not be surprised if we experience this communion as paradoxical.

If these paradoxes ring a bell in our own experience, this means that at some important moments in life each one of us has experienced something that lies at the very core of the monastic vocation. It means that the monastic quest is not at all as foreign to us as we might tend to think. In fact, it means that our personal experience gives us an inside access to what makes monastic life tick. Anyone who can say from experience "When I lose myself, I'm truly myself," understands from within what moves a person to choose a life of detachment. To understand does not mean to be called to do the same; that's obvious. Yet, it will help us place monastic life in perspective. Anyone who knows our second paradox from experience—"When I'm truly alone, I'm one with all" and "When I'm one with all, I'm truly alone"—knows the seed experience from which a life of celibacy grows. Anyone who has experienced that "When I drop the question, the answer is there"—and who hasn't experienced this in some moment of grace?—is familiar with the paradox that lies at the very root of obedience.

These paradoxes are like the seed. The goal of monastic life is the harvest this seed yields. What lies between the seed and the harvest is asceticism. Yet, the harvest of monastic life is the fruit of ascetical effort, not its result. There is a difference. "Even though the farmer cares and labors," says Rilke, "Where the seed is turning into harvest,/He never reaches. *Earth bestowes*" (*Sonnets of Orpheus* I:12). Neither is the yield of monastic life an achievement, "but something given/And taken, in a lifetime's death in love/Ardour and selflessness and self-surrender" (T. S. Eliot; *Four Quartets* 3:V). But the harvest is always the same as the seed, only more of it. And so, to know the seed-experience goes a long way to help us understand what monks and nuns are all about in their ascetical labors.

Between the thrill of losing yourself and so being for one moment truly yourself, and the enduring joy of selfless living lies a lifetime of self-surrender in detachment, a life of voluntary poverty, as Christian tradition calls it. We tend to think of voluntary poverty as giving up things. But that is partly an exercise in detachment and partly an expression of detachment. Detachment as such does not consist in stripping ourselves of possessions. It consists in stripping ourselves of selfishness. After we have given away everything, we can still remain attached to our very detachment, and we will be no better off than if we had held on to material possessions. Worse, in fact. For it is easier to notice that we are on the wrong track when we hold on to obviously perishable things, than when we make an idol out of our would-be virtues. Only when I am detached even from my detachment do I habitually live in that freedom that I breathed for a moment when I lost myself and so found my true Self.

A life of voluntary poverty cultivates that freedom we felt in our Peak Experience by a variety of means. The whole monastic environment is designed to facilitate this process of progressive detachment. It's an affectionate detachment. A letting go, gently. Not a throwing away. Never are things as splendid as at the moment when we lovingly give them up. That is why to someone who visits a monastery for the first time, the simplest things of everyday use often seem to radiate an inexplicable beauty. Should this surprise us? Should not a spoon or a bowl which generations of monks washed after each use as if this had been their last meal somehow radiate that mindfulness? Mindfulness. That is the key to a life of detachment. Monks and nuns keep cultivating mindfulness and all the different ascetical practices of voluntary poverty have only one goal: to make us more mindful.

Thoughtlessness takes things for granted. Mindfulness makes grateful. Gratefulness makes happy. That is why a good monastery is a place where happiness is at home. No matter how much we possess, if we take it for granted it will only add to our boredom. But no matter how little we have, if we are mindful of the fact that everything is a gift, everything will make us thankful and so inspire the joy of gratitude. In fact, the less we can call our own, the easier it becomes to see the preciousness of this given world in which we live. In a monastery one cultivates this joy of grateful detachment by becoming more mindful. A novice might have to start by closing doors mindfully, by turning off lights when leaving a room, by treating books with reverence, by not letting the faucet drip, or by parking a pair of sandals neatly rather than pigeon toed or right-foot-left. It is amazing how strands of monastic tradition separated by thousands of years and tens of thousands of miles agree in some of these seemingly ridiculous details. And everywhere newcomers chafe at the bit to get beyond what they consider minor details to the more spectacular forms of self-stripping, unaware that mindfulness is all that matters, the mindfulness of that liberating moment in which we lose ourselves and so find our Self.

There is a link here with our second paradox. The Self I discover in the flash of mindfulness, which is my Peak Experience, is paradoxically both one with all and alone. My experience of liberation at that moment springs from the discovery that having lost myself, I have nothing left to lose. As Janis Joplin sings: "Freedom's just another word for nothing left to lose." But I also realize in a flash that nothing I lose can be lost, for I am one with all. To whom could I lose it? When I'm truly alone, I'm one with all, and when I'm truly one with all, I'm alone. This aloneness is not the loneliness of the individual cut off from all others, but the solitude of the person intimately belonging to all. So all-including is this belonging that it leaves exclusive relations behind. And here lies the root of celibacy, a root that even those not called to a celibate life can trace in their own experience and appreciate.

There are those whom that glimpse of belonging to all in solitude stirs into a lifelong quest for its full realization. For them, the asceticism of celibacy lies between the seed of the mystical spark and the steady flame of pure, all-embracing love. This asceticism of celibacy has many forms and many stages. It is a process of growth. It has its own setbacks, struggles, growing pains and joys. Its basic movement is from exclusive belonging to universal belonging and from loneliness in isolation to solitude in community. A community supporting solitude is, of course, only one kind of community, an exceptional kind to be sure. Yet, that is what a monastery offers. Not to recognize monastic community as solitude community would lead to grave misunderstandings, yet this could easily happen. For in a good monastery the bonds of friendship are so strong and the atmosphere of love is so striking that it takes a second look to realize the goal, which is not togetherness but mutual support in solitude. While this is most clearly seen in the monastic setting, it holds true in varying degrees for every community of celibates.

The means by which the celibate life is fostered in the monastic environment are twofold. They remind one of the two-fold means we use in teaching a child to swim: we support and we leave alone. Everything depends on the right balance between these two ways of assistance at a given moment. Community life in a monastery depends on the alertness of every member for the needs of every other in this respect. Monks or nuns are the guardians of each other's solitude. They must protect it, on the one hand, against interference and, on the other hand, against deterioration. At any moment solitude is apt to deteriorate into loneliness unless there is someone at hand to provide loving support. Yet, this support must be given in the attitude of lovingly giving the other one up, without clinging, without possessiveness. (It goes without saying that giving up is the very opposite of letting down.) It is a mothering attitude with which celibates uphold each other and set each other free. At the edge of the monastery lies the hermitage; sometimes geographically, sometimes in a more hidden form. Monastic training is always training for solitude; that's what the very term *monastic* implies. The great friendships of monastic history are its most beautiful fruits. They prove the fact that genuine friendship is never exclusive but creatively expanding into wider and wider community. They show us men and women whom friendship supports in being so gracefully alone that they are fully one with all, celibates who have become so deeply one with all that solitude is the only adequate expression of their universal belonging.

Now, just as the first paradox we experienced in our mystical moment—when I lose myself, I find my Self—is the seed from which a life of voluntary poverty springs, and the paradox of being alone, yet one with all, lies at the root of celibate life, so the paradox that the answer is there the moment I drop the questions gives rise to a life of obedience.

Unfortunately, the first thing that comes to mind when we hear the term *obedience* is doing what someone else tells you to do. But this is merely one form of the ascetical practice that here, too, lies between the seed and the harvest. The seed, as we saw, is the experience of a wholehearted "Yes" in response to reality. This is what we should think of when we speak of obedience in the full sense. Immediately we understand that there is more to that than doing what you are told to do. First of all, we must learn to listen, to really expose ourselves to the message, to try and understand it. We must learn to have the courage to respond, learn to adjust our "Yes" to the message, so it won't just be a reaction but a genuine response. And all this in confrontation with a host of things and persons in a bewildering variety of situations. It is no easy task. Obedience in the limited sense in which it is usually understood is an attempt to make that task easier by simplifying the setting.

In a well-ordered monastery no one need be in doubt about what ought to be done at any given time. This alone simplifies the situation greatly. It is a learning situation. The monastery is a training ground for obedience. The training starts out with some plain do's and don't's and may lead to the most excruciating exposure to "the word of God, living and efficient and keener than any two-edged sword, extending even to the division of soul and spirit, of joints and marrow, and discerning the thoughts and intentions of the heart" (Heb. 4:12). There is no set method or course for this learning process, no grades or lessons. The monastic environment provides the setting for a progressive tuning in on the Word of God spelled out moment by moment in the persons one encounters, the things one handles, the situations in which one finds oneself. A seasoned monk usually guides the novice, but only so far. The goal is independence, inner freedom, freedom above all from the enslavement to self-will, prejudice, and preconceived notions. No more effective way towards that freedom has yet been invented than the practice of voluntarily handing over one's decisions for a time to a trusted spiritual guide. That is the monastic way.

The goal of obedience is to stand on one's own feet and to give one's own free response to the call of each moment. It is in this responsible freedom that a human person comes fully alive. The monastic path is only one possible way towards this goal, but a well-tried one. The fullness of life to which it leads is simply experienced as peace of heart. That is, after all, what every human being is longing to find. And let us note that peace of heart does not so much depend on external circumstances. There are people who have everything one could wish for, and yet lack that peace of heart that others have found in the midst of misery. What is it then that makes for peace of heart? The answer is: to find meaning in life. If we find that, our peace of heart is assured; if we cannot find it, life is absurd. But this little word *absurd* gives us an important clue. The Latin word *ab-surdus* from which it derives means "absolutely deaf." Its exact opposite is *ob-audiens*, from which our word *obedience* came, and that means "thoroughly listening." The very language we use suggests the basic choice that lies before us in life: absurdity or the responsive listening of loving obedience.

"I set before you today life and death, blessing and curse, says the Lord. Choose life!" (Deut. 30:19) This is how the Bible puts the matter of our basic choice. Let us be very careful not to identify this most basic choice with the choosing of a particular form of life. But let us be equally careful not to separate the two completely. Monastic life is only one form in which life and blessing is offered to us. All that matters for me is whether or not it is the form to which I am personally called. But if I am called, all my happiness in life will depend on choosing this particular path. How can I know whether or not I am called? What question should I ask myself in order to find out?

Let us remember that God normally speaks to us clearly enough through circumstances. We never need to wait for a little voice whispering into our ear from somewhere! "Do this!" If we merely apply common

sense to our concrete circumstances and listen to the response of our innermost heart (you have to be very still to
hear it), God's word will come through to us strong and
clear. This holds true for any vocation.

We must also remember that our choice cannot be based
on finding the most direct path among all others or the
objectively best, or highest, or holiest form of life. If any
objective standards of that kind can at all be established,
they are, at any rate, of secondary importance in so personal
a decision. What is at stake is your personal happiness and
peace of heart. If you keep this in mind it is obvious what
question you ought to ask yourself in order to determine
your calling. The question is simply "What will give me
peace of heart?" God is a God of peace. He calls us to "Seek
peace and pursue it" (Ps. 34:15). No path can promise us the
happiness that comes from good luck. But the path that
appeals to your heart as most deeply meaningful does promise to sustain you regardless of external circumstances.

It seems that men and women of all times and all over the
world experience those moments of meaning to which we
have referred as Peak Experiences. And it also seems that
those moments have great significance for the orientation of
our lives towards Ultimate Meaning and for the basic choices
we make. The ways of cultivating the seed of those experiences will vary from culture to culture, from person to
person. Forms which look totally different may still be
inspired by the same seed and lead to the same harvest. What
counts in our context is that throughout the ages there have
been men and women—few and far between for the most
part—who invented and cultivated monastic forms of life
and so created traditions specially designed to foster a
professional approach to our common human quest for

meaning. Voluntary poverty, sexual abstinence and training in obedience are invariably key elements in these traditions, among whom the various forms of Christian monastic life are merely one chapter.

It helps us place the monastic vocation in its proper perspective if we remember that it is not primarily a Christian, but a basic human phenomenon. If we could watch the history and prehistory of monastic life as we know it today compressed into a filmstrip of one hour, the whole Christian era would have to be fitted into the last five minutes. And even throughout the last two thousand years Christian monks and nuns have at best been a significant minority among their non-Christian brothers and sisters—Hindu, Buddhist, Jain and others. This gives them an important position. It makes them quite naturally the bridge-builders between the universal human quest for meaning in its most articulate form and the Good News of meaningful life in Christ. Monks and nuns all over the world speak the same language, as it were. In the things that really matter, they are often much closer to each other across religious boundaries than they are to lay people of their own respective religious groups. This makes monasteries the ecumenical centers of the future, even without any explicit efforts to this effect. The greatest value monasteries offer to our human family today may well lie in the witness they bear to the unity of the human quest for Ultimate Meaning.

Of course, the Good News adds more than mere trimmings to the perennial monastic endeavor of the human race. In the light of the Gospel, monastic life is rediscovered and reinterpreted from within. What Christians call the evangelical counsels, voluntary poverty, celibacy, and obedience, are the age-old pillars of monastic life now built into the edifice of the Church. Detachment becomes a radical response to the call of Jesus, who says, "If you want to be perfect, go and sell all you have and give the money to the poor, and you will have riches in heaven; then come and follow me" (Mt. 19:6). Celibacy is now seen as the state of those of whom Jesus said that they "do not marry because of the Kingdom of heaven. Let him who can do it accept this teaching" (Mt. 19:12). And training in obedience becomes in the Christian context a way of growing up in Christ, who "even though he was God's Son learned to be obedient by means of his sufferings" (Heb. 5:8). It would be obviously wrong to say that anyone who takes Christ's call seriously has to follow the monastic path. But it is true that some people have to do so, because their God-given personality calls for this form in order to find its highest fulfillment. Had they been born in a different part of the world, that same disposition would have made them candidates for Buddhist or Hindu monastic life. Christian monastic life springs up wherever the seed of the Gospel is sown into a heart that by its characteristic makeup will find peace only through a professionally contemplative life.

At different periods and in different places people have created different environments to foster their contemplative life. Monastery differs from monastery even within the same religious order. Often a vocation is inseparable from one's attraction to a particular monastery, its location, its history, even its architecture and its climate. Still there are certain striking similarities between otherwise incomparably different places, say a Buddhist monastery in Thailand and a Benedictine abbey in Italy, or a Tibetan Lamasery and a Comaldolese hermitage on the Big Sur coast. For one thing, we are dealing in each of these cases with an artificial environment, set up by an intentional community. I have called it a professional environment, a laboratory. St. Benedict, the patriarch of Western monks, calls it a workshop and a school. At any rate, it is an environment designed with a clear purpose in mind, and that purpose is the same wherever a monastery is established, namely to orientate everything, down to the smallest detail, to the pursuit of mindful living. In a most comprehensive way, space and time are, therefore, different in a monastery from what they are anywhere else.

Even a casual visitor to a monastery is apt to sense in some vague way that there is something special about that place, and that time seems to stand still. We could put it a different way by saying that the place is holy ground and the time is sacred time. But what does this mean? Surely it isn't a statement on the level of geography or chronometry. What makes the difference is heightened awareness, mindfulness. When the voice of God from the burning bush calls out to Moses, "Take off your shoes; this is holy ground!" (Ex. 3:5), Moses becomes aware of God's awe-inspiring presence. But God is present everywhere. Wherever we take off our shoes, we stand on holy ground. Monks spend a lifetime taking off their shoes, removing what comes between their life sensitivity and that part of the world with which they should be in touch then and there. This may express itself in a preference for unpainted wood, for plain food, for getting one's hands soiled with honest dirt once in a while. But it goes deeper. It is a spiraling process. The use of simple things makes monks more mindful. And having become more alert to God's mysterious presence, they learn to make things, design buildings, grow gardens, in such a way that others who use these things or live in these spaces are, in turn, made more mindful—until the whole place helps you to be truly present where you are—and that isn't so easy.

One reason why we are so seldom really present where we are is that we have no time. We are constantly rushed, at once ahead of ourselves and getting behind. One of the first things one learns in a monastery is to do things when it is time. One bell or another will tell you when it is time for this or that. And then you can devote yourself fully to the task at hand until it is time for something else. It takes a bit of discipline to let one thing go at the stroke of a bell and to turn to a new task, but it is truly liberating. Suddenly time is no longer a strictly measured succession of so many seconds per minute and so many minutes per hour, impersonally counted out by a ticking timepiece. Time has become something new: opportunity for encounter—here and now—potentially a chain of Peak Experiences, of timeless moments. "Only through time time is conquered" (T. S. Eliot, *Four Quartets,* 1:II).

This kind of time and space makes the monastery the setting for prayer without ceasing. By this we do not mean multiplying of prayers, but rather living life in grateful awareness of God's presence. That awareness is prayer. It lifts everything up into the sunshine of God. In Christian tradition the monastery is the ever-present mountain of Christ's transfiguration where time and space become transparent for the light of God's glory.

Yet, in our world his glory is paradoxically a hidden glory, and that paradox is the paradox of the cross. When Jesus descended from the mountain after the Peak Experience of his transfiguration, he said to his disciples: "Tell no one of the vision you have seen, until the Son of Man is risen from death" (Mt. 17:9). This means that we cannot bypass the cross. It will loom large in every monastic vocation, both in the personal lives of monks and nuns and in monastic life as an institution. The way in which the cross appears in our personal lives will always be unexpected. The surprise aspect is an essential element of the experience whenever the shadow of the cross falls on our path. Not much more can be foretold about it. We might be able, however, to trace in rough outline the shadow that dims the splendor of monastic institutions within the Church of North America at this present time. To do so seems only fair when writing for people who might have a monastic vocation. But there is another reason for doing so. In any living movement problems push toward solutions. And the monastic movement is certainly alive among us today. To gauge the pressures at work within it might allow us to see a dim outline of the solutions the future is likely to bring. The cross always points toward Easter morning.

The decisive pressures reshaping Christian monastic institutions in North America today spring directly from the thrust of the monastic quest itself. In our time, as in age after age before us, the human need for a contemplative environment asserts itself and is groping for new forms adjusted to a new situation which offers new challenges and opportunities. There are two pressure centers in this process: one within the existing monastic institutions, where monks and nuns continue to strive for growing faithfulness to their calling; another one on the outside, where lay people have discovered that they, too, have a contemplative life that needs to be fostered, and now press for some share in monastic forms. This pressure from without is far less noticeable than the pressure from within. It is far less strong and less concentrated. But it is widespread and of considerable significance, for it is felt by sensitive and alert persons and seems to have a future.

The thrust within monasteries takes a two-fold direction: on the one hand, towards greater solitude and a generally more strictly ascetical life; on the other hand, toward sharing the fruits of contemplative life through apostolic service. These two directions are only apparently incompatible, since our civilization offers for the first time sufficient social and economic flexibility for individuals to go back and forth between the most austere monastic setting and most any area of service and apostolate. Hence, there are now monks and nuns who question why they should spend their whole life in one and the same setting, especially if that setting proves to be a sort of middle ground, not really meeting the crying needs of our time for outgoing service (and rightly so, for a monastery is not designed to do that), but not being intensely ascetical either (and this because of problems arising from monastic stability).

Stability in a monastic vocation has traditionally been identified in the Western Church with lifelong residency within cloister walls. This always entailed the danger of mediocrity. If there is no way of taking a break, the intensity of the effort will be lowered to a level so easygoing that no break is needed. Today, a second problem is added: stability of residency entails the need to earn one's living while in the monastery. In many instances this is found today to necessitate so much involvement in business that the quality of the contemplative environment is seriously threatened. It seems that these pressures tend to reshape the notion of stability from a static to a dynamic one. It may well be that in the future monasteries will be looked at as places where people spend periods of intense contemplative life, interspersed, according to one's personal needs, with periods during which one goes out to serve and, incidentally, also earn one's livelihood. While there may always be people who manage to spend their whole life fruitfully and honestly within cloister walls, the notion of stability in one's vocation seems to be evolving today from residential stability to a stability of unswerving commitment. This is the direction in which both the pressure from within and the pressure from without seem to push for release.

The moment a monastic community is no longer defined as the group in residence, but comprises also those who have at the time gone out to serve and earn, there is no reason why this community should not be expanded to include all those who somehow or other "belong" to that monastery, whether they are professed monks and nuns who at times go out, or lay people who at times come in. This could even eliminate the pressure of monastic hospitality to guests, who tend at times to weigh down by their sheer numbers the monasteries to which they flock until the contemplative life of the place is in jeopardy. (It is one thing to have children come home for vacation and quite a different thing to entertain visiting uncles and aunts.) Stability and hospitality are the major areas of pressure on today's monastic scene. What we see happening promises release for both of them at once and so seems indeed to hold some promise for the future and allows us to glimpse some outline of what monastic life might be like when today's novices will be seasoned monks and nuns.

Much of this is guesswork. What is certain is merely that there will be monastic life as long as human beings respond to the yearning of their heart to make the quest for meaning (for Ultimate Meaning, for God) their primary concern, and to go about it with professional earnestness. They will always be few, but all that counts here is quality, not quantity. A handful of monks and nuns can serve as catalysts for a whole society. Former times spoke of this catalytic function as witnessing. The monastic witness keeps alive in the Church the tradition of the prophets and the martyrs. Monks and nuns fulfill, thus, within the Church a function comparable to that which the Church fulfills within society as a whole. They are reminders of the urgency to distinguish between wants and needs; the urgency to reflect before we rush into action; the urgency to find beyond the multitude of purposes in which we are engaged the meaning that will give us peace of heart.

It should be obvious from all this that one cannot choose a monastic vocation, just as one cannot choose to be a prophet or a martyr. But there have always been, and there are, those who hear the call and say, "Here I am!"

Mirror of the Heart

Haiku poetry in itself is an inexhaustible topic. To discover it, to enter more deeply into it, to revel in its delights would be worthwhile in itself. But what I would like to consider here is the function of the Haiku as a mirror. Like a crystal, the facets of which mirror and bring together so many different reflections of the world around it, the Haiku shows us some important aspects of the world of man gathered together and reflected as if in one brief sparkling flash. The clarity and precision of this remarkable poetic form is only heightened by the fact that it is so utterly unsentimental. So is a mirror.

The Haiku as mirror for human self-understanding will have its function whenever this self-understanding tends to get blurred. Yet, in our time it may be particularly helpful. For one thing it is an Eastern form of poetry reaching the West precisely at the moment when one great task before us is bridge-building between East and West. And it is a poem of awareness. Among all poetic forms there is not one in which awareness is more central than in the Haiku, and this at a time when we are discovering new horizons of awareness both in outer and in inner space. In this awareness, the Haiku never loses sight of the paradox of time and space, and this, too, makes it particularly helpful for our own new self-awareness. For as men like Einstein and T. S. Eliot have pointed out to us from very different vantage points, the paradox of time and space lies at the core of our new confrontation with the paradox of man.

The Haiku thus becomes a many-faceted mirror in which we may look for deeper understanding of the human paradox. And this suggests the way in which we might go about building this essay. We must begin with experience, your own experience, if possible, and so on the outset we shall try to get to some experience of your own—one of those experiences in which the human paradox comes to a peak. We shall explore this Peak Experience in the hope of discovering some key aspects for a deeper understanding of it. T. S. Eliot will help us in this, for he faces directly, and in a way that is more familiar to Westerners, the same paradox that the Haiku reflects indirectly. This will be our next step: to examine just how the various aspects of the human paradox are reflected in the crystal of the Haiku.

We shall let the Haiku speak for itself as far as possible, but as we listen to it and allow ourselves to swing with it, we shall become aware of its preponderance toward one pole of our experience—its "still point." And this shall provide us, unexpectedly, for some maybe, with a key for understanding monastic life. Surprising as the connection between Haiku and monastic life may appear, it stands on solid ground. The human paradox discovered in the peak experience, and crystallized in the Haiku, is lived out in monastic life as one of its paradigmatic forms. This is what provides the connection. Man's new self-understanding, for which our time is groping and towards which the Haiku can help us, is simply incomplete without the contemplative dimension, or to put it more concretely, without the discovery of the monk in each one of us.

But we have a long way to go, and we must start, as we have said, with experience, and this as close to home as possible with a peak experience of your own. The term *Peak Experience* is a good one, and a useful one. For we do experience our lives as relatively long stretches of ascent and decline culminating here and there in brief moments for which a peak is the perfect image. But like every term, the term *Peak Experience* lends itself to empty manipulation, and this would be futile. To use the term well, we must fill it with content from the well of our own experience. We are setting out on an exploration of inner space—your own, and we won't settle for less.

May I suggest, then, that you take your eyes off the page at this point. Closing your eyes, you might recall and relive one of those major or minor peaks of your past experience. Try to focus on a moment of which you can truly say that it made your life worthwhile, not for others (this would put us on the wrong track here) but for yourself. Seen from one of these peaks, the long stretches of ascent were suddenly meaningful, the slopes of decline appeared bearable: life was seen as worth living.

Maybe it was even outwardly a moment on a mountain top, at sunset, it could be, or in the brisk brilliance of an autumn day. Maybe it was a passage in a book, a poem, or a melody that lifted you up onto an inner peak, unnoticed by anyone else. Or sitting on a fence rail dangling your legs, not in boredom, not at all, but in utter absorption. Absorption into what? Into nothing; for nothing happened. And those moments mark our highest peaks, those moments when nothing does indeed happen to us. If this last point puzzles you, don't give up too quickly. All that matters for the moment is that you set your mind on a Peak Experience of your own, a specific one against which you can check my suggestions. For I will suggest, in outline, some aspects of the dynamic event which took place at that moment. You must check for yourself how this outline applies.

What makes it so different to reflect on the moment of our Peak Experience is that it is in itself an altogether unreflexive moment. This is, in fact, its main characteristic. What makes the *Peak Experience* so liberating is that precisely for once I no longer feel that I feel and know that I know but simply feel and know and just that. Only afterwards can I reflect on it and so talk about it. And what I am then inclined to say is something like "I was simply swept off my feet," or "I was out of myself, carried away." Even though it might have been for a split second only, "I had lost myself." This was all. But not quite all. For looking back I will so admit that at the moment of my Peak Experience I was more truly and more fully myself than at any other time. And so I find myself confronted with the strange paradox that I am most truly myself when I forget myself. When I lose myself, I find my Self.

This paradoxical tension between self and Self, between losing and finding, is paralleled (and this is the second aspect) by another facet of the paradox and you can check this too against your own experience. It matters little whether the experience you have in mind took place on a lonely mountain, or, say, in the midst of a crowded concert hall. At the peak moment you were alone in a deep sense. Not that you were reflecting on it then and there, but reflecting on it later you find that the word *alone* applies, even though there may have been a crowd around you. You were in some sense "the only one." You were, and this is even more important, not only singled out but of a single mind; and so you were "alone" also in the sense of being altogether with yourself, all of one piece, "all one."

But this second facet of our paradox also implies attention. Precisely as you were all one with yourself, you experienced keenly being one with all. Your profound solitude was matched by limitless togetherness. In fact, the two were simply two aspects of the same experience. And again it matters little whether externally you were alone or in a crowd. Even alone on an island, miles away from other human beings, you may have been overwhelmed by the awareness of a deep union with everyone. Nor was this togetherness limited to people. At this melting point your innermost being had fused into the fragrance of the wild thyme in the evening meadow, into the sudden flash of winter lightning, into the voice of the waterfall or of the flute. You were alone, all one, one with all.

There was nothing to be said at that point. It is only afterwards that we are putting all of this into words, limping words at that, words that will never catch up with our experience. But in some sense you yourself were a word at that crucial moment, a word more simple and immediate than words are once they have surfaced into language. This word will necessarily lose in translation but if we must attempt translating it, what comes closest might be simply "Ah!" or "Wow!" or "Yes!" or "This is it!"—an exclamation of awe-filled affirmation. You had somehow gone beyond reasoning and suddenly everything made sense. This is a third facet of our paradoxical Peak Experience. No questions asked, no answers given, and yet everything appears right, just as it is. Chinese wisdom caught this insight in a saying which is as simple as it is deep: "The beautiful snow never falls onto an inappropriate place." Indeed, this is merely a more elaborate way of saying "This is it!"

When I exclaim "This is it!" the meaning of "it" is simply without limit. It means life and death, it means the whole universe and it stretches out to anything that may lie beyond it. It stands for ultimate meaning. And yet what I have discovered is not an abstraction but this concrete thing before me, a thing that is meaningful, full of meaning, and so I am never quite sure of where to put the accent of my "This is it!" The emphasis hovers between "This is IT!" on the one hand, and "THIS is it!" on the other. A moment ago we stressed the "IT," the overpowering meaning revealed in our experience. Now we stress the "THIS," the thing or situation at hand in all its concreteness. And by this switch we realize that the meaning is not, as it were, behind this thing, or above, or beyond, or inside it. The thing or situation is simply a word or sign that embodies its significance. It is simply the shape of its meaning. This fragrance of wild thyme, this tone of a flute is simply one shape of Ultimate Reality. I cannot decide where to place the accent. All I am sure of is that "This IS it!"

I hope that you were able to check these aspects of a Peak Experience step by step against your own. Yet all this is still mere talk about experience, and I apologize. Poets don't talk about an experience. They let it come to word. That's quite a different way of approach, and this is where we come to Haiku.

Much must be presupposed here, and much may be presupposed, for excellent introductions to Haiku poetry are easily available in English. But through our reflections on the Peak Experience, we have gained access to Haiku from

within, as it were. If you have become aware that you are
most truly yourself when you forget yourself; that in truly
being alone you are one with all; that everything makes sense
as soon as you go beyond reasoning; you have discovered in
your own experience the paradox in which Haiku has its
roots.

Not that the Masters of Haiku would try to "capture" a
Peak Experience (a Western poet might try to do this); what
they are trying to do is not to capture the experience, but to
set it free—to stimulate you just barely enough to bring back
an experience of your own. A master of Haiku will make the
reader his co-poet. "We had the experience but missed the
meaning." Now, seen in the mirror of Haiku, "the hint half
guessed, the gift half understood..." that had been granted
to us at last yields its meaning. The poet offers you a mirror,
but a mirror without light is empty and dark. The light that
flashes in the crystal mirror of Haiku must be the light of
your own experience.

But here we are already in the midst of paradox. Did we
not say that you had "lost yourself" at the climax of your
Peak Experience? Where were you when you were "swept
off your feet?" Nowhere and everywhere. How then can the
Haiku bring you back to the place that was no place? To that
time that was out of time? It does so, paradoxically, by
bringing you to a most specific place at a most specific time.
(Here lies, incidentally, the importance of the so-called
"season word" of classical Haiku.) Vagueness is incompatible with Haiku, because it is altogether incompatible with
"the sudden illumination" of the Peak Experience. And the
"season word," far from being a literary convention, aims at
that bursting of space and time which, paradoxically, coincides with the ultimate clarity and precision of the here and

now. It is a strange coincidence that the English word *nowhere* is a fusion of *now* and *here*. "You cannot face it steadily," but if, for one brief now you are truly here (wherever this may be), you are nowhere because you are everywhere.

> Here, the intersection of the timeless moment
> Is England and no where, never and always.

How, then, can the Haiku help you recover "the point of intersection of the timeless with time"? The point where "all is always now"? How? Simply by leaving room. Not by what is said, but by what is left unsaid. This Hiaku, for instance, takes shape just at the point where reflection returns, and I, reentering the orbit of my little self, become aware that I had gone beyond.

> THE BUTTERFLY HAS DISAPPEARED AND NOW
> IT COMES BACK TO ME, MY WANDERING MIND.

Who is to capture the moment in which you have lost yourself? The moment of which reflexive awareness can take hold is only the moment after, the moment of return—from where?

> I can only say, there we have been; but I
>   cannot say where.
> And I cannot say, how long; for that is to
>   place it in time.

And what is it that "comes back to you"? Is it the butterfly or your wandering mind? We are left in suspense. Who can tell in the end? Who needs to tell?

All this may have taken place in a flash. But in another Haiku, the poet suggests a losing of self in wonderment, sustained, maybe, for hours throughout a moonlit night.

> THE MOON IN THE PINES
> NOW I HANG IT UP, NOW I TAKE IT OFF
> AND STILL I KEEP GAZING.

Again that delicate suspense which here pivots on the little word "still." Is it in stillness that I am gazing? Am I still gazing on and on after "hanging" the moon on this branch or that? Or, and this to me is the most intriguing possibility. am I still gazing after having taken down the moon, gazing at nothing, and still gazing?

But just to make sure that moon and butterflies and the moods they evoke are not at all essential to the kind of experience that concerns us here, let me give you a very different one still in the context of losing oneself. Here the setting is refreshingly active: rows of farm workers hoeing fields on a distant hill, rhythmically swinging their mattocks.

> UP THEY SWING
> AND THE MATTOCKS GLITTER:
> FIELDS IN SPRING.

What a virile image of spring. That fraction of a moment in which the sun flashes on a shining blade, here and now sparks an explosion of power and joy, bursting your little self, capitulating you to that "still point" where "ALL IS ALWAYS NOW."

It takes only a slight shift of emphasis, and the point of aloneness in dynamic stillness becomes the point of consummate union. The butterfly, in whose flight I had lost myself, unified my vision, for by taking me out of myself, it made me one with all, and healed me of duality. And now that almost imperceptible shift of emphasis:

> DOWN THE BARLEY ROWS
> STITCHING, STITCHING THEM TOGETHER
> THE BUTTERFLY GOES.

In a moment of celebration, this butterfly restores aloneness to all-oneness. As I am watching it, stitching the barley rows together, I lose myself and realize the profound paradox hinted at by the English word "alone—"all-one." To be truly alone is not at all to be lonely, for the heart of my heart, that secret place where I am most intimately myself, is, paradoxically, the point where I am also the most intimately one with all other human beings, with all living being, with all that has being. To be truly alone is to be healed of duality, one with my true Self, and thus one with all.

To be alone in this sense is to have reached what T. S. Eliot calls "the still point of the turning world," the still point of the Great Dance, the peak "where past and future are gathered."

> Neither movement from nor towards
> Neither ascent nor decline
> Except for the point, the still point
> There would be no dance, and there is
> Only the dance.

Let us look at another Haiku:

FIVE BLUE BUTTERFLIES
SUMMER ROADSIDE FESTIVAL
DUSTY BOOTS STAND STILL.

Here, again, the meaning pivots on the ambiguity of the words "stand still." Is this an imperative? Is the poet saying, "For heaven's sake, here it is, the Great Dance. It doesn't take more than a handful of those commonest of all butterflies, the tiny blue ones rarely seen on flowers, but content to put on their summer festival on the ruts of dirt roads running through summer fields. Here it is, the still point of the Great Dance, and it is all yours if only you will stand still!" Or is this again a fully accomplished instance of self lost and Self found, the all-oneness of the solitary traveler whose dusty boots stand still, at long last, "at the still point of the turning world," "and there is only the Dance"?

THE LAKE IS LOST
IN THE RAIN WHICH IS LOST
IN THE LAKE.

THEY BLOSSOM, AND THEN
WE GAZE, AND THEN THE BLOSSOMS
SCATTER, AND THEN...

The pain of blissful aloneness, and the bliss of the pain that makes all one, keenly coincide in the peak of the Peak Experience, in the still point, in the Haiku.

The moments of happiness...
We had the experience but missed
    The meaning,
And approach to the meaning restores
    The experience
In a different form, beyond any meaning
We can assign to happiness...

Pain and bliss are reconciled, all opposites are reconciled, and we are reconciled to the paradox that the opposites coincide. Duality is not eliminated but healed, overcome in solitude-togetherness. Without argument, without reasoning everything suddenly makes sense. We can say "Yes" to paradox.

But this is not a "Yes" of resignation. It is a "Yes" of triumph, an unlimited "Yes" of reality, to Ultimate Reality. It is a "Yes" pregnant with newness of discovery. Our ears are popping; our eyes pop open and see all the familiar things as if we had never seen them before:

> GREEN FIELDS OF GRAIN:
> A SKY-LARK RISES OVER THERE.
> COMES DOWN AGAIN.

> AS THE SPRING RAINS FALL,
> SOAKING IN THEM, ON THE ROOF,
> IS A CHILD'S RAG BALL.

This freshness of vision may rise to a crescendo of surprise at the most ordinary things. So in the wildest of all the Haiku I know: here the overabundance of cherry blossoms so fills the poet with sobering inebriation that he looks even at horses and birds as if it were for the first time in his life.

> CHERRY BLOSSOMS, MORE
> AND MORE NOW! BIRDS HAVE TWO LEGS!
> OH, HORSES HAVE FOUR!

The directness and immediacy that is so overpowering here is possibly the most striking characteristic both of the Peak Experience and of the Haiku. No abstractions here!

THEY ROLLED OUT TOO FAR
FROM THEIR LEAF SHELTER, MELONS—
AND HOW HOT THEY ARE!

TRUCKLOADS OF PUMPKINS
SWISHING BY. AND IN THE DUST
ONE BUSTED PUMPKIN.

One melon, one pumpkin—we see it, we feel it, our whole being says "Yes, this is it", and we have said "Yes" to the whole universe. What is more marvelous; that the meaning of the whole universe gives itself to us in one pumpkin, or that one pumpkin can convey to us the meaning of the whole universe? We need not decide. The marvel lies in the coincidence of the two: that ultimate meaning should be so concrete and that this concrete thing should be so ultimately meaningful.

Between the lightning flash seen and the impact of its meaning perceived, there must not be the slightest crack or crevice into which reflexive thinking could insert itself. This would destroy the immediacy of the experience. This is the burden of Basho's famous statement: "When the lightning flashes, how admirable he who does NOT think: life is fleeting." To think it would mean to "over-stand" rather than "understand," grasp one aspect of the experience rather than being "grabbed" by its total impact. Understanding hinges on the directness of our insight, "This IS it!"

It is with the meaning revealed in the Peak Experience that the Haiku is ultimately concerned. Not, of course, and this should be clear from all that we have said, as if the meaning could be separated from the word that gives it expression. The meaning is not another word behind the word. Meaning is silence. It comes to itself as it finds form. It finds form as it comes to word, but meaning, as such, is silent. And "words after speech reach into silence."

The Haiku is, paradoxically, a poem about silence. Its very core is silence. There is probably no shorter poetic form in world literature than the classical Haiku with its seventeen syllables and, yet, the masters put these seventeen syllables down with a gesture of apology, which makes it clear that the words merely serve the silence. All that matters is the silence. The Haiku is a scaffold of words; what is being constructed is a poem of silence; and when it is ready, the poet gives a little kick, as it were, to the scaffold. It tumbles, and silence alone stands.

> EVENING RAIN
> THE BANANA LEAF
> SPEAKS OF IT FIRST.

We can almost hear the first big raindrops falling one by one. But this is already the moment after the decisive one; the moment after the one that held its breath in limitless anticipation. This is not a poem about rain, but about the silence before the rain. A strange poem, the Haiku! It zeroes in on the here and now which is nowhere. It celebrates the all-oneness of aloneness in all the bliss of its poignant pain. It stakes out territory for discovery precisely where life is most daily. And while setting up landmarks of adventure, it wipes out its own footprints. It denies itself. For it shoots words like arrows at the target of silence. Every word that hits the mark returns to that silence out of which it has come.

Does this sound paradoxical? It certainly is, yet, no more paradoxical than you are to yourself. For the Haiku merely mirrors the paradox of the "still point"—the paradox of the human heart. In a masterly Haiku what it means to be human has been crystallized. Crystallized, not petrified. Not like rock, but lightly as in a snowflake that will melt and become a drop of water as soon as it touches you. Crystallized in the Haiku, the paradox is not dispelled. It is brought home; it is made bearable; you can stand under it and rejoice in it as children rejoice in snowflakes. And thus, standing for once under the paradox rather than over against it, you can understand; you can understand yourself.

Self-understanding attained at the "still point"; this is the core of the Peak Experience; the burden of T. S. Eliot's *Four Quartets*; the hidden source of Haiku poetry; the goal of the monk. Of course, the goal is the same for all of us, and monastic life is but one possible way of attaining this goal. But in its form, monastic life is paradigmatic, allowing us to trace the human paradox in a few broad strokes.

This is the reason why in man's identity crisis, today, many turn with renewed interest toward monastic tradition. Those whose interest turns in this direction will hardly be able to find a more direct approach to understanding monastic life than the one attempted here. For as long as we try to find access to it from the outside, we won't get beyond highly complex socio-religious phenomena in history; we won't get beyond labels. But approached from within, along the lines suggested here, the monastic quest will be seen to be much more than a periodically recurring fringe phenomenon of organized religion. It will reveal itself as one possible way of realizing a basic human dimension, the exploration of inner space; something pursued by few but in behalf of all; something that concerns each one of us. And, in a measure, it can be understood by every human being.

If you have experienced

> ... The moment in and out of time,
> The distraction fit, lost in a shaft of sunlight,
> The wild thyme unseen, or the winter lightning
> Or the waterfall, or music heard so deeply
> That it is not heard at all, but you are the music
> While the music lasts....

If you have experienced, no matter how marginally, the painful bliss of it all, why not concede the possibility that others might attempt to center their whole life on this one goal:

> ... To apprehend
> The point of intersection of the timeless
> With time...

(They may be eccentrics, granted. In fact, one might have to be eccentric in order to feel so strong a need for zeroing in on this center "at the still point." So what? A need is always the reverse side of a talent.)

And if you have experienced the rich aloneness that, though it be for one moment, only dissolves all limits to your oneness with the universe, why not concede the possibility that someone may choose to become a "loner" for the sake of becoming a "brother" to brother wolf and to brother sun, to sister water and to sister death? (After all, *monachos* means literally "loner," and yet, it is the monk whom everyone calls "brother.")

And, again, if you have seen in a flash that everything makes sense as soon as you go beyond reasoning, you will be ready to understand why some men and women should devote their whole life to the pursuit of this paradox. What they are seeking is:

... Not the intense moment
Isolated, with no before and after,
But a lifetime burning in every moment.

... But to apprehend
The point of intersection of the timeless
With time, is an occupation for the saint—
No occupation either, but something given
And taken, in a lifetime's death in love,
Ardour and selflessness and self-surrender.

For most of us, this is the aim
Never here to be realized;
Who are only undefeated
Because we have gone on trying;

For us, there is only the trying,
The rest is not our business.

The road of monks is but one of the possible roads of
approach to the "still point," but it is an approach by which,
for a long time, many have made their way. And while some
basic experience of the human paradox is necessary to understand the forms of monastic tradition from within, the forms
of life that the monks have cultivated may in turn aid us in
our understanding of the human paradox.

As we have seen, the human paradox flares up in a sudden
flash of self-understanding "at the still point" of the Peak
Experience. It happens. No effort we could make would
earn for us this experience. It is gratis: *gratia gratis data*— a
gift, always. What, then, can we do towards it? We can
prepare ourselves. And how? The monk's answer is: by
training. An ascetic is one who trains. (The Greek word
askein means "to exercise," and since this exercise is directed
towards a goal, "to train.") This is what asceticism is: goal-

directed systematic training. And the goal is to discover, again and again, "the still point."

No wonder, then, that some decisive strokes, characteristic for the ascetic tradition, should correspond to lines we have been able to trace in the Peak Experience. Thus, we shall encounter again the paradox of a here and now intensified beyond space and time. The particular form this paradox assumes in ascetic life is "detachment" (never to be confused with indifference). We shall also find again the paradox of solitude and togetherness, and its particular form will be ascetic "celibacy." And we shall meet again the "this-is-it" experience in all its paradoxical tension. The peculiar accentuation of this tension characteristic of ascetic life gives rise to a whole life style marked by silence, mindfulness, prayer, celebration. What lies at the root of this life style is "obedience"—in a much more comprehensive sense, obviously, than obedience has in everyday language— obedience as a constantly renewed listening to the meaning of each moment. All three—detachment, celibacy, and obedience— are directly related to the quest for the "still point."

We have said "detachment," but any connotation of indifference must be completely ruled out. Any resemblance between indifference and detachment is mere deception. For detachment is not a withdrawal from love, but an expansion of love beyond desire. Desire is entangled in time, nostalgic for the past, preoccupied with the future. Love expanding beyond desire is "liberation from the future as well as the past." What remains is the Now "where past and future are gathered," the "still point."

In our own daily life we may experience the liberating expansion of love. In fact, we may come to find our own little action increasingly unimportant and yet of ever-increasing significance as the context in which they are seen expands. This is what happens along the way of monastic detachment: the here and now gains in significance precisely in proportion to the loss of its importance. "At the still point" here and now cease to matter and attain ultimate significance. A "secluded chapel," a "winter's afternoon" become "England and nowhere. Never and always." This implies that training in detachment must aim at cultivating its own awareness of space and time. Nothing short of this will do.

The various forms by which monks of different traditions cultivate the ascetic approach to space, for instance, may appear poles apart from one given case to another. But once we have the clue, it is easy to see that the goal is the same. Forms as different from one another as the homelessness of the pilgrim monk and stability in the cloister are merely two ways to the same goal. A wayfaring monk on the roads of India, or a stylite who spends his life on a pillar; the Irish monks of the Middle Ages seafaring across the northern Atlantic or the walled-in recluses in ancient Russia; and all those monks whose form of life falls somewhere between these extremes—they all simply aim at this: being present where they are—truly, totally present.

> . . . In order to arrive there,
> To arrive where you are, to get from where you are not,
> You must go by a way wherein there is no ecstasy.

"Ecstasy" literally denotes a "being beside oneself," put out of place, even deranged—the very opposite of that total centeredness, that full presence where you are, with both feet on the ground, in a given "instant." That the "ecstasy" should happen at the very "instant" is merely the linguistic reflection of the paradox with which we are here concerned. There is the ecstatic instant, but there is no instant ecstasy. Monastic training is unhurried and down to earth: sweeping, cooking, washing; serving at table or at the altar; reading books or filing library cards; digging, typing, haying, plumbing—but all of this with that affectionate detachment which makes the place where you are the navel of the universe.

To this monastic awareness of place belongs a distinctively monastic awareness of time.

> The time of the seasons and the constellations
> The time of milking and the time of harvest.

The time of "the sea bell's perpetual angelus" on the coast where

> The tolling bell
> Measures time not our time, rung by the unhurried
> Ground swell, a time
> Older than the time of chronometers, older
> Than time counted...

And the "unhurried ground swell" becomes an image of that "love expanding beyond desire," detached but not indifferent, on the contrary, alert and responsible—for the time measured by the tolling bell is "not our time." We are called. We must respond.

> And the ground swell, that is and was from
>   the beginning,
> Clangs
> The bell.

The angelus bell and the gong, the clapper, the drum, the sounding board are so many ways of keeping time "not our time." This is the decisive point: that it is "not our time."

The monks rise and go to sleep, work and celebrate, when "it is time." They are only "keeping" the time, not "setting" it. At the first sound of the bell, the monk is to let loose whatever he is engaged in, and turn to that for which it is time. What matters is the letting loose. It is liberation. Through it the time which was "not our time," all time, becomes ours because we give ourselves to it. Swinging with the living seasons you are "in tune with the world," and it is all yours.

This detachment from time and place through which everything becomes ours because we are fully present in the here and now, this is the seed fruit of monastic detachment, its ultimate accomplishment containing in seed everything.

> A condition of complete simplicity
> (Costing not less than everything.)

All other renunciation is included in the monk's affectionate detachment from the here and now. It points to that ultimate self-detachment in which our true Self is found.

> In order to possess what you do not possess
> You must go by the way of dispossession.
> In order to arrive at what you are not
> You must go through the way in which you are not.

Detachment, understood in this truly catholic, i.e., all-embracing sense, leads us directly to monastic celibacy, because

> Love is most nearly itself
> When here and now cease to matter.

Celibacy certainly belongs in the context of "expanding of love beyond desire, and so, liberation." Seen in this light, the accent switches from the aspect of dispossession, deprivation, renunciation to the aspect of expansion, liberation, fulfillment. In the context of the Peak Experience it makes sense to say that the monk is a celibate, a loner, because his oneness with all is expanding beyond desire. And it is equally true to say that he can embrace this oneness with all only because (and in so far as) he is truly alone. Celibacy is the daring attempt to sustain the "condition of extreme simplicity" in which solitude and togetherness merge so that aloneness becomes all-oneness.

This experience of concord with oneself and with all, a concord realized at the heart of the universe, at the still point—this experience is always granted gratis. But it is one thing to be surprised by it in a flash in the "moment of happiness ... the sudden illumination" and quite a different thing to sustain a life centered on this still point, to remain "still and still moving." For this we need the support of others embarked on the same venture. (Even the hermit needs this support, though less tangibly.) Monastic solitude must be supported by togetherness.

It is surprising how much togetherness one needs to save aloneness from deteriorating into loneliness. Here lies the root of monastic community. Solitude and togetherness make one another possible. Take away solitude and togetherness becomes subhuman gregariousness; take away togetherness and solitude becomes desolation. Community can only exist in the tension between solitude and togetherness. The delicate balance between solitude and togetherness will determine what kind of community it shall be. In the togetherness community of which married life is the prototype, togetherness is the measure of solitude: each partner must have as much solitude as he needs for rich and full togetherness. In the solitude community of monastic

life, solitude is the measure of togetherness: here each partner must have just enough togetherness to enrich and support his solitude. Monks in community help one another in
love to cultivate and sustain genuine aloneness.

No one can do without this support. Even the solitary
explorer must still rely on the team that stands behind him.
The stakes of this exploration are high. Celibate life means

> . . . a trip that will be unpayable
> For a haul that will not bear examination.

Supported "at the still point" we must explore the togetherness dimension of solitude, the all-oneness of aloneness.

> We must be still and still moving
> Into another intensity
> For a further union, a deeper communion
> Through the dark cold and the empty desolation.

> We shall not cease from exploration
> And the end of all our exploring
> Will be to arrive where we started
> And know the place for the first time.

We shall "know," but to know in this way shall be "the
haul that will not bear examination." It will be a kind of
knowledge that goes beyond count, beyond measure; not a
knowing of knowledge, but a knowing experience.

> . . . There is, it seems to us,
> At best, only a limited value
> In the knowledge derived from experience.

What monks are after is not "knowledge derived," but
immediate knowledge; not the knowledge we can grasp, of
which we can take hold, but the meaning that speaks to us in
the experience, hits us, "grabs" us, takes hold of us. And just

as we saw that "time, not our time" gives itself to us as soon as we let loose in detachment and give ourselves over to its liberating power, so the meaning for which we are searching in life gives itself to us as soon as we renounce the effort to grasp it and begin to listen to it. Knowledge tries to grasp; wisdom listens. Listening wisdom: that is obedience.

Obviously, obedience here is taken in its most comprehensive sense. We must not restrict obedience to the notion of "doing someone else's will." This may be a somewhat conspicuous aspect of monastic training, yet submission is not an end in itself. It is a means, and only one of various means. The end is obedience in its full sense as a loving listening to the meaning that comes to us through everything and every person and every situation. If obedience meant no more than doing someone else's will, it might merely replace my own whims by the whims of someone else, but monastic training is designed to liberate from whim altogether. The master helps the monk to become detached from self-will, but this is only the beginning. The real task is learning to listen. The very word *obedience* comes from *ob-audire*, which means to listen intently. Its opposite is to be utterly deaf, and the word for this is literally *ab-surdus*. Everything is absurd until we learn to listen to its meaning; until we become "all ears" in obedience.

In order to listen, you have to be silent. Silence, then, is another means towards the intent listening of obedience. We mean an inner silence, above all, but this implies an outward silence which expresses and supports the inner. Yet, monastic silence does not consist in the elimination of words, the elimination of noise. This process of elimination leads, at best, to the hush of a public library or of a morgue. Monastic silence is not dead silence; it is alive with the presence of mystery like the silence of a deep forest. It is like the silence of a forester totally mindful of the game he is stalking. And all this recollected silence is intent on one goal: "to apprehend the point of intersection of the timeless with time"—the still point.

Monastic mindfulness of recollection, like monastic silence, is directly related to obedience. It is not the grim *memento mori* as which it is sometimes seen. And yet, it is truly "mindfulness of death, because death is precisely the ultimate point of intersection of the timeless with time." But the recollection of the monk is not a morbid preoccupation with one's last hour. It is mindfulness of the present hour, the here and now, the "intersection time," and it is in this sense that "the time of death is every moment." At any moment in which you are truly present, the breakthrough through the time barrier may occur through recollected consciousness. The moment of total presence, through recollection, is "the moment in and out of time." Thus "history is a pattern of timeless moments." Through recollected mindfulness, practiced throughout a lifetime, whatever the present moment contains becomes "a symbol, a symbol perfected in death." In monastic life everything becomes "a symbol" because we are learning to listen to its meaning.

Prayer is unlimited mindfulness. And this coincides with the most traditional notion of prayer while it broadens the concept immensely. For you have always known that you can "say your prayers" without really having prayed. And when we ask: "what is it then, that makes prayers, prayer?" The answer is "recollection." (Mindfulness means the same, but the term is less worn by use and abuse.) If you say your prayers mindfully, you really pray. Well then, what really matters is obviously mindfulness, recollection, openness. The gesture of the open hands, raised in prayer, is typical in contrast to the clenched grip that tries to hold onto things.

Prayerful recollection is loving openness to receive the meaning conveyed by a given moment. Set times for prayer are certainly necessary to cultivate prayerfulness, but should we restrict prayer to set times? If we know what it means to say prayers mindfully, we ought to be able to do everything with the same mindfulness. And thus everything becomes prayer; everything becomes celebration. Everything becomes celebration as we learn to take things one by one, moment by moment; to single everything out for grateful consideration.

Seen in this light, prayer, too, is but another way of listening in obedience. Submission, silence, recollection, prayer, what holds all these ascetic practices together is obedience. Detachment makes the monk free for the "trip that will be unpayable." Celibacy is the way in which he sets sail. Obedience is the lifelong voyage of exploration.

Monastic life, in solitude community, is only one way, not the only one. We have said this before. A married man or woman might someday outline in a similarly paradigmatic form how the self-finding in a self-losing, the paradox of oneness and aloneness, and the listening for the silent meaning of life express themselves in togetherness community. The points of resemblance with monastic life might turn out to be stunning. When you look at a circle of dancers from outside the circle, those nearest to you will seem to move in one direction, those farthest from you in the opposite one. Yet, contrary to appearance, all of them are moving in the same direction around the circle.

> And the way up is the way down, the way
> forward is the way back.

All that matters is the still point of the dance.

A Deep Bow

People often ask me how Buddhists answer the question "Does God exist?"

The other day I was walking along the river. The wind was blowing. Suddenly I thought, oh! the air really exists. We know that the air is there, but unless the wind blows against our face, we are not aware of it. Here in the wind I was suddenly aware, yes it's really there.

And the sun too. I was suddenly aware of the sun, shining through the bare trees. Its warmth, its brightness, and all this completely free, completely gratuitous. Simply there for us to enjoy.

And without my knowing it, completely spontaneously, my two hands came together, and I realized that I was making gassho. And it occurred to me that this is all that matters: that we can bow, take a deep bow. Just that. Just that.*

—THE REVEREND EIDO TAI SHIMANO

If we were able to experience this fundamental gratitude at all times, there would be no need to talk about it, and many of the contradictions that divide our world would at once be resolved. But in our present situation, talking about it might help us at least to recognize this experience when it is granted to us, and give us courage to let ourselves down into the depth which gratitude opens up.

---

*From a recent address by the Reverend Eido Tai Shimano, a Japanese Zen Master who teaches at the Zen Studies Society in New York.

We can begin by asking ourselves, "What happens when we feel spontaneously grateful?" (It is, of course, this concrete phenomenon which concerns us here, not any abstract notion.) For one thing, we experience joy. Joy is certainly there at the basis of thankfulness. But it is a special kind of joy, a joy received from another person. There is that remarkable "plus" which is added to my joy as soon as I perceive that it is given to me by another, and necessarily another person.

I can treat myself to a delicious meal, but the joy will not at all be the same as if someone else treats me to a meal, even though it be a little less exquisite. I can prepare a treat for myself, but by no means of mental acrobatics can I be grateful to myself; there lies the decisive difference between the joy that gives rise to gratitude and any other joy.

Gratitude refers to another, and to another as person. We cannot in the full sense be grateful to things, or to impersonal powers like life or nature, unless we conceive of them in some confused way as implicitly personal, super-personal, if you wish.

The moment we explicitly exclude the notion of personality, gratitude ceases. And why? Because gratitude implies that the gift I receive is freely bestowed, and someone who is capable of doing me a favor is by definition a person.

A joy, even though I receive it from another, does not make me grateful unless it is meant as a favor. We are quite sensitive for the difference. When you get an unusually big piece of pie in the cafeteria, you may find yourself hesitating for a moment, and only when you have discarded the possibility that this may indicate a change of policy or an oversight, you take it to be a favor worthy of a smile for the fellow that hands it to you across the counter.

It may be difficult in a given case to say whether the favor I receive was meant for me personally. But my gratitude will depend on the answer. At least the favor must be meant for a group with which I am personally identified. (When you wear a monk's habit you not infrequently receive a bigger piece of pie or some other unexpected kindness from someone you never met before and whom you will never meet again. But there, the people do mean you, insofar as you are a monk, and it is quite a different case from the painful experience of smiling back at someone only to discover that the smile was meant not for you but for someone who stood behind you.)

Where does this little phenomenology of gratitude lead us? That much we can already say: gratitude springs from an insight, a recognition that something good has come to me from another person, that it is freely given to me, and meant as a favor. And the moment this recognition dawns on me, gratitude, too, spontaneously dawns in my heart: *Je suis reconnaissant*—I recognize, I acknowledge, I am grateful; in French these three concepts are expressed by one term.

I recognize the special quality of this joy: it is a joy freely granted to me as a favor. I acknowledge my dependence, freely accepting as a gift what only another, as other, can freely give to me. And I am grateful, allowing my emotions fully to taste and to express the joy I have received, and thus I make it flow back to its source by returning thanks. You see that the whole man is involved when he gives thanks from his heart, from that center in which the human person is one: the intellect recognizes the gift as gift; the will acknowledges my dependence; the emotions, like a sounding board, give fullness to the melody of this experience.

The intellect recognizes: yes, it is true, this joy is a free gift; the will acknowledges: yes, it is good to accept my dependence; the emotions resound in gratitude, celebrating the beauty of this experience. Thus, the grateful heart, experiencing in truth, goodness and beauty the fullness of being, finds through gratitude its own fulfillment. This is the reason why a person who cannot be wholeheartedly grateful is so pitiful a failure. Lack of gratitude always indicates some malfunctioning of intellect, will or emotions that prevents the integration of the personality thus afflicted.

It may be that my intellect insists on suspicion and does not allow me to recognize any favor as favor. Selflessness cannot be proved. Reasoning about another person's motives can only take me to the point where mere intellect must yield to faith, to trust in the other, which is a gesture no longer of the intellect alone but of the whole heart. Or it may be that my proud will refuses to acknowledge my dependence on another, thus paralyzing the heart before it can rise to give thanks. Or it may be that the scar tissue of hurt feelings no longer allows my full emotional response. My longing for pure selflessness, for pure gratitude, may be so deep and so much in discrepancy with what I have experienced in the past that I give in to despair. And who am I anyway? Why should any selfless love be wasted on me? Am I worthy of it? No, I am not. To face this fact, to realize my unworthiness, and yet to open myself through hope to love, this is the root of all human wholeness and holiness, the very core of the integrating gesture of thanksgiving. However, this inner gesture of gratitude can only come to itself when it finds expression.

Expression of thanks is an integral part of gratitude, no less important than the recognition of the gift and the acknowledgment of my dependence. Think of the helplessness we experience when we do not know whom to thank for an anonymous gift. Only when my thanks are expressed and accepted is the circle of giving and thanksgiving closed and a mutual exchange established between giver and receiver.

However, the closed circle is not a well-chosen image for what happens here. We could rather compare this exchange to a spiral in which the giver receives thanksgiving, and so becomes himself receiver, and the joy of giving and receiving rises higher and higher. The mother bends down to her child in his crib and hands him a rattle. The baby recognizes the gift and returns the mother's smile. The mother, overjoyed with the childish gesture of gratitude, lifts up the child with a kiss. There is our spiral of joy. Is not the kiss a greater gift than the toy? Is not the joy it expresses greater than the joy that set our spiral in motion?

But notice that the upward movement of our spiral signifies not only that the joy has grown stronger. Rather we have passed on to something entirely new. A passage has taken place. A passage from multiplicity to unity: we start out with giver, gift and receiver, and we arrive at the embrace of thanks expressed and thanks accepted. Who can distinguish giver and receiver in the final kiss of gratitude?

Is not gratitude a passage from suspicion to trust, from proud isolation to a humble give and take, from enslavement to false independence to self-acceptance in that dependence which liberates? Yes, gratitude is the great gesture of passage.

And this gesture of passage unites us. It unites us as human beings, for we realize that in this whole passing universe man is the one who passes and knows that he passes. There lies our human dignity. There lies our human task. The task of entering into the meaning of this passage (the passage which is our whole life), of celebrating its meaning through the gesture of thanksgiving.

But this gesture of passage unites us in that depth of the heart in which being human is synonymous with being religious. The essence of gratitude is self-acceptance in that dependence that liberates; but the dependence which liberates is nothing else but that religion that lies at the root of all religions, and even at the root of that deeply religious (though misguided) rejection of all religions.

When we look at the great rites of passage that belong to man's oldest religious heritage, the religious significance of gratitude becomes clear to us. In recent years anthropologists and scholars of comparative religion have made much of these "rites de passage," rites celebrating birth and death and the other great hours of passage through the human life. Sacrifice in one form or another belongs to the core of these rites. And this is understandable, for sacrifice itself is the prototype of all rites of passage.

The moment we take a closer look at the basic features common to the various forms of sacrificial rites, we are struck by the perfect parallel between the structure of gratitude as a gesture of the human heart and the inner structure of sacrifice. In both cases a passage takes place. In both cases the gesture rises from the joyful recognition of a gift received, culminates in an acknowledgement of the receiver's dependence on the giver, and finds its accomplishment in an external expression of thanks which unites giver and receiver, be it in the form of a conventional handshake of gratitude, or in a sacrificial meal.

Think, for example, of the sacrifice of first fruits, almost certainly the most ancient sacrificial rite. Even where we find it in its simplest and most primitive form the rite clearly displays the pattern we discovered. Let us take, for example, the Chenchu, a tribe in Southern India, belonging to one of the most ancient cultural strata not only of India but of the whole world. What happens when a Chenchu returning from a food-gathering expedition in the jungle casts a choice morsel of food into the bush and accompanies this sacrifice with a prayer to the deity worshipped as mistress of the jungle and of all its products? "Our mother," he says, "by your kindness we have found. Without it we receive nothing. We offer you many thanks."

Thousands of similar rites have been observed among the most primitive peoples. But this example (recorded by Christoph von Fuerer Haimendorf, who did field work among the Chenchu) stands out for its crystal clear structure. Each sentence of the simple prayer accompanying this offering corresponds, in fact, to one of our three phases of gratitude. "Our mother, by your kindness we have found": the recognition of a favor received; "without it we receive nothing": the acknowledgement of dependence; and "we offer you many thanks": the expression of gratitude that makes the original joy over the favor received rise to a higher level.

And what the prayer expresses under three aspects, the rite expresses in one gesture: the hunter who offers a piece of his quarry to the deity expresses thereby that he appreciates the goodness of the gift received, and that through the symbolic sharing of the gift he somehow enters into communion with the giver.

So striking, in fact, is the correspondence between social gestures of gratitude and religious gestures of sacrifice that one might tend to mistake the food offerings of the Chenchu and similar examples for a mere transposition of social conventions into a religious key. However, there is no simple dependence of the one on the other. Both are rooted in the depth of the heart, but they expand in two different directions.

Man's religious awareness comes to itself through the very gesture of his sacrificial rites, just as his awareness of human solidarity comes to itself when one man expresses his thanks to another.

Man looks at life and sees that it comes to him from a Source far beyond his reach. He looks at life and sees that it is good—good for him: and from the firm ground of these two intellectual insights the heart dares to leap to a third insight that surpasses mere reasoning: the insight that all good comes to me as a free gift from the Source of Life. This leap of faith surpasses the groupings of the intellect, because it is a gesture of the whole man, very much like the trust I put in a friend.

Now, the moment I recognize life as a gift, and myself as recipient, my dependence is brought home to me, and this confronts me with a decision. Just as in the social sphere I can refuse to acknowledge dependence, and lock myself up in the loneliness of pride, so in the religious dimension I can adopt a stance of proud independence towards the very Source of Life. And the temptation is strong to close my eyes to the ridiculousness of this posture. For dependence in the religious context implies more than the give and take of human interdependence; it implies obedience to a Being greater than I. And my petty pride finds it hard to swallow this.

(It is here, incidentally, that the violence of many sacrificial rites has its root. We cannot do justice to this aspect now, but we may note in passing that violent sacrificial rites are meaningful as an expression of that violence which we must do to ourselves before our hearts, enslaved by self-will, can enter into the freedom of loving obedience.) The man who kills an animal in sacrifice expresses by this rite his own readiness to die to everything that separates him from the goal of this rite of passage. Since the goal is union between the human and the divine, a union of wills must precede it; the human will must become obedient. But the death of self-will is only the negative aspect of obedience; its positive aspect is man's birth to true life and joy. Upon the immolation follows the joy of the sacrificial banquet.

We should not overstress submission when we speak of obedience. Of much greater importance is the positive aspect: alertness to the secret signs pointing the way towards true joy. (I call them secret signs because they are intimately personal hints, in moments when we are most truly ourselves.) "We, unlike birds of passage, are not informed," says Rilke in the *Duino Elegies*. Our passage is not predetermined by instinct. All we are given are inklings like that stirring of gratitude in our hearts, and the freedom to follow these inklings.

To the extent to which we have forfeited this freedom, detachment is necessary. Obedience is our alertness, our *disponsibilité*, our readiness to follow the homing impulse of the heart in its upward flight. Detachment liberates the wings of our heart so that we can rise to the grateful enjoyment of life in all its fullness. We must open our hand and let loose what we hold before we can receive the new gifts that every moment offers us. Detachment and obedience are merely means; the goal is joy.

If we would understand moral sacrifice in this positive way we would also understand ritual sacrifice, which is its expression. Neither of the two is that grim thing into which it is sometimes distorted. The pattern of both is the passage of thanksgiving. The accomplishment of both is the joy of man's union with that which transcends him. This is expressed in the sacrificial banquet in which the rite of sacrifice culminates. This joyful meal presupposes the acceptance of man's thanksgiving by the divinity. It is the embrace which unites the one who gave the gift and the one who gives thanks for it.

(Let us remember, by the way, that in the religious context, God is always the giver: man is the thanks-giver. Only in the far less original context of magic can this relation deteriorate to some sort of commercial transaction or even to man's effort to extort favors from super-human powers. But magic and ritualism are dead-end roads of the heart; they do not concern us here.)

What does concern us is the fact that our own experience of gratitude is closely related to a universal religious phenomenon, to sacrifice, which lies at the very root of religion. And once we have grasped the root, we can find access to religion in all its aspects. The whole history of religion can, in fact, be understood as the working out in all its implications of that sacrificial gesture that we ourselves experience as often as gratitude rises in our hearts.

Jewish religion, for example, begins with the implicit conviction that man would not be man unless he offered sacrifice, and leads up to the explicit awareness that "only one who brings himself as sacrifice deserves to be called man" (Rabbi Israel of Rizin, who died in 1850). We have a perfect parallel in Hinduism where an early Vedic text sees man as "the one animal capable of bringing sacrifice," (*Satapata Brahmanah* VII, 5, 2, 23) and the development culminates in a passage from the *Chandogya Upanished* (III, 16, 1): "Verily, a person is a sacrifice." Does not our own experience show us that a human person finds his own integrity only in the sacrificial gesture of thanksgiving?

And even to the "thou shalt love" (which is in one form or another the mature fruit of every religion) does our experience of gratitude give us access. But just as the root repelled us at first by its apparent crudeness, so this fruit of religion makes us draw back from the contradiction it seems to contain. How can love be commanded? How can there be an obligation to love? Love is not love at all unless it is gratuitous. What we experience in the context of gratitude provides us with a clue: a favor we do to another remains a favor, remains gratuitous, even though our heart tells us that we ought to do it, that we ought to be generous, ought to pardon. And why? Because we belong together in a deep solidarity that the heart discerns. We belong together, because together we are obligated to a reality that transcends us.

Christ's word comes to mind: "If you are offering your gift at the altar, and there you remember that your brother has something against you, leave your gift there before the altar, and go. First make peace with your brother, then come and offer your gift" (Mt. 5:24). This is in perfect conformity with the tradition of Israel's prophets who insisted that true sacrifice is thanksgiving, that true immolation is obedience, that the true meaning of the sacrificial meal is mercy, *hesed*, the convenant, love, which binds men and women to one another by binding them as one community to God.

What is rejected is empty ritualism, not ritual. Thanksgiving, mercy, obedience are not to replace ritual, but to give it its full meaning. Indeed, man's whole life is to become a sacred ritual of thanksgiving, the whole universe a sacrifice. When the prophet Zachariah says that "on that day" (the day of the Messiah) "every pot and pan in Jerusalem and Judah shall be sacred to the Lord of hosts, so that all who sacrifice may come and use them," the implication is that there is nothing on earth that cannot become a vessel filled with man's gratitude and lifted up to God.

It is this universal *Eucharistia*, this cosmic celebration of a thanksgiving sacrifice that forms the heart of the Christian message. And even to those of us who are not Christians the experience of gratitude gives at least a speculative access to the Christian belief that the spiral of thanksgiving is the dynamic pattern of all reality, that within the absolute oneness of the triune God there is room for an eternal exchange of giving and thanksgiving, a spiral of joy. Within the one and undivided Godhead, the Father gives himself to the Son, and the Son gives himself in thanksgiving to the Father. And the Gift of Love eternally exchanged between Father and Son is himself, personal and divine, the Holy Spirit of Thanksgiving.

Creation and redemption are simply an overflow of this divine *perichorese*, this inner-trinitarian dance, an overflow into what of itself is nothingness. God the Son becomes the Son of Man in obedience to the Father, so as to unite through his sacrifice in merciful love all men with one another and with God, leading them back in the Spirit of Thanksgiving to that eternal embrace in which "God will be all in all" (I Cor. 13: 28). "Whatever exists, exists through sacrifice" (*Sat. Brah.* XI, 2, 3, 6). The whole cosmos is being renewed moment by moment through sacrifice: brought back to its source through thanksgiving and received anew as gift in all its primordial freshness. But this universal sacrifice is possible only because the one God, himself, is Giver, Thanksgiver, and Gift.

To those among us who have entered into this mystery through faith it need not be explained; to others, it cannot be explained. But to the extent to which we have given room in our hearts to gratitude, we all have a share in this reality, by whatever name we may call it. (It is a reality that we shall never fully take hold of. All that matters is that we let it take hold of us.) All that matters is that we enter into that passage of gratitude and sacrifice, the passage which leads us to integrity within ourselves, to concord with one another and to union with the very Source of Life. For ". . . this is all that matters: that we can bow, take a deep bow. Just that, Just that."